1

This book belongs to:

_____

Sagittarius Daily Horoscope 2025

Author's Note: Time set to Coordinated Universal Time Zone (UT±0)

Mystic Cat
Suite 41906, 3/2237 Gold Coast HWY
Mermaid Beach, Queensland, 4218
Australia
islandauthor@hotmail.com

Contents

The 12 Zodiac Star Signs

2025

January

S	M	T	W	T	F	S
			1	2	3	4
5	6	7	8	9	10	11
12	13	14	15	16	17	18
19	20	21	22	23	24	25
26	27	28	29	30	31	

February

S	M	T	W	T	F	S
						1
2	3	4	5	6	7	8
9	10	11	12	13	14	15
16	17	18	19	20	21	22
23	24	25	26	27	28	

March

S	M	T	W	T	F	S
						1
2	3	4	5	6	7	8
9	10	11	12	13	14	15
16	17	18	19	20	21	22
23	24	25	26	27	28	29
30	31					

April

S	M	T	W	T	F	S
		1	2	3	4	5
6	7	8	9	10	11	12
13	14	15	16	17	18	19
20	21	22	23	24	25	26
27	28	29	30			

May

S	M	T	W	T	F	S
				1	2	3
4	5	6	7	8	9	10
11	12	13	14	15	16	17
18	19	20	21	22	23	24
25	26	27	28	29	30	31

June

S	M	T	W	T	F	S
1	2	3	4	5	6	7
8	9	10	11	12	13	14
15	16	17	18	19	20	21
22	23	24	25	26	27	28
29	30					

July

S	M	T	W	T	F	S
		1	2	3	4	5
6	7	8	9	10	11	12
13	14	15	16	17	18	19
20	21	22	23	24	25	26
27	28	29	30	31		

August

S	M	T	W	T	F	S
					1	2
3	4	5	6	7	8	9
10	11	12	13	14	15	16
17	18	19	20	21	22	23
24	25	26	27	28	29	30
31						

September

S	M	T	W	T	F	S
	1	2	3	4	5	6
7	8	9	10	11	12	13
14	15	16	17	18	19	20
21	22	23	24	25	26	27
28	29	30				

October

S	M	T	W	T	F	S
			1	2	3	4
5	6	7	8	9	10	11
12	13	14	15	16	17	18
19	20	21	22	23	24	25
26	27	28	29	30	31	

November

S	M	T	W	T	F	S
						1
2	3	4	5	6	7	8
9	10	11	12	13	14	15
16	17	18	19	20	21	22
23	24	25	26	27	28	29
30						

December

S	M	T	W	T	F	S
	1	2	3	4	5	6
7	8	9	10	11	12	13
14	15	16	17	18	19	20
21	22	23	24	25	26	27
28	29	30	31			

2025

Daily Horoscope

SAGITTARIUS

As your astrologer, I wish to explain why one horoscope book may differ from another for each zodiac sign. The vast array of astrological activity constantly occurring in the sky requires me to focus on the essential aspect of the star sign I am writing for on any given day. Each zodiac sign is unique, and the various planetary factors affect them differently.

When crafting horoscopes, I pay special attention to the significant astrological aspects directly impacting a specific sign. By doing so, I can provide the most insightful and relevant guidance to individuals of that zodiac sign. While there might be multiple planetary alignments on a particular day, one aspect may hold more significance for a specific sign than others.

Considering the ruling planets and elements associated with each zodiac sign further refines my interpretations. This attention to detail ensures that the horoscope resonates with the distinct characteristics and tendencies of the star sign in question.

Ultimately, I aim to offer personalized insights and advice based on each zodiac sign's unique cosmic influences. By focusing on each star sign's most relevant astrological aspects, I can help readers better understand themselves and navigate the energies surrounding them. Embracing each zodiac sign's strengths, challenges, and opportunities allows me to create a horoscope book tailored to my readers' needs.

"We are born at a given moment, in a given place, and, like vintage years of wine, we have the qualities of the year and the season of which we are born. Astrology does not lay claim to anything more."

—Carl Jung

JANUARY

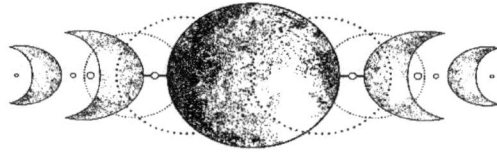

MOON MAGIC

Sun	Mon	Tue	Wed	Thu	Fri	Sat
			1	2	3	4
5	6	7	8	9	10	11
12	13	14	15	16	17	18
19	20	21	22	23	24	25
26	27	28	29	30	31	

NEW MOON

_____

_____

_____

_____

_____

_____

_____

_____

_____

_____

_____

_____

_____

_____

_____

_____

_____

_____

_____

_____

_____

_____

WOLF MOON

30 Monday

With the moon ingressing Capricorn and the new moon's arrival, you can build a solid foundation and take a disciplined approach toward your ambitions. It's a time to evaluate your long-term plans and make practical choices that align with your values. Structure and organization blend with a desire to progress in your endeavors. This New Moon offers an opportunity for you to lay the groundwork for future success and make steady progress toward your aspirations.

31 Tuesday

New Year's Eve brings a sense of anticipation and excitement as you reflect on the past year and look forward to the new one. The social aspect of your life is expanding, and it's time to connect with others. Communication is vital, and as you develop personal ties, you'll find that abundance and new opportunities are all around you. This chapter will be colorful and full of social opportunities, opening up new possibilities and soul-stirring experiences.

1 Wednesday

On New Year's Day, with the Moon entering Aquarius, a sense of innovation and open-mindedness fills the air. It's a time to embrace your unique qualities and express your individuality. You may feel inspired to break free from convention and explore new ideas and perspectives. This lunar influence encourages you to connect with like-minded individuals and collaborate to promote progress and positive change.

2 Thursday

As life heads towards an upward trajectory, you land in an environment ripe with possibilities. You set sail on a timely voyage that expands your life outwardly. Nurturing your life hits a sweet spot that draws abundance into your world. A situation you invest time and energy into blossoms into a path forward. It ushers in a more connected and supportive environment. It sets the stage for an expressive and happy time.

3 Friday

As Venus enters Pisces, it heightens sensitivity and compassion in your relationships. It encourages you to tap into your intuition and embrace the beauty of selfless love. Meanwhile, the opposition between Mars and Pluto brings intensity and transformation. This aspect can be a time of power struggles and conflicts, but it also offers an opportunity for profound personal growth and empowerment.

4 Saturday

As the Sun forms a sextile with Saturn, you can harness your discipline, focus, and determination to achieve your goals. This harmonious aspect supports you in taking practical steps toward long-term success and stability. You may find yourself more responsible and reliable, willing to put in the necessary effort and work diligently towards your aspirations. This transit encourages you to embrace structure and organization, making overcoming obstacles easier.

5 Sunday

With the Moon entering Aries, you may feel energy and assertiveness in your emotional landscape. This fiery and bold influence inspires you to take action and enthusiastically pursue your desires. You are encouraged to embrace a proactive and confident approach, allowing your instincts to guide you. This lunar transit ignites a sense of independence and self-assurance, empowering you to assert your needs and initiate new beginnings.

6 Monday

With Mars entering Cancer, you may notice a shift in energy and drive. This influence brings a focus on home, family, and emotional matters. You might feel more motivated to nurture and protect those you care about, creating a sense of emotional security. However, with Mercury square Neptune, there could be a tendency for confusion and misunderstandings in communication. Being mindful of your thoughts is essential, as this transit has illusionary energy.

7 Tuesday

With the Moon entering Taurus, you may experience a deep sense of stability and groundedness in your emotions. This transit encourages you to prioritize comfort, security, and material well-being. You draw life's simple pleasures and may find solace in indulging your senses and enjoying the physical world. This aspect is a time to nurture yourself and create a sense of inner harmony by surrounding yourself with beauty and engaging in activities that bring you peace and serenity.

8 Wednesday

With Mercury entering Capricorn, you may notice a shift in your thought patterns and communication style. Your focus turns to practicality, efficiency, and long-term goals. You approach conversations and decision-making with a more structured and organized mindset. Your thoughts become more logical and strategic as you seek to make practical and well-thought-out choices. This transit encourages discipline and focus, emphasizing clarity and precision.

9 Thursday

With the Sun in Capricorn gracing your second house, your disciplined nature is directed towards matters of finance, values, and self-worth. You approach material security with a strong work ethic and a keen sense of responsibility. Financial stability is a focus, and you find fulfillment in building a solid foundation through careful planning and strategic investments. Allow yourself to find a balance between responsibility and enjoying the fruits of your labor.

10 Friday

With the Moon entering Gemini, your emotional energy becomes more curious and communicative. You draw social interactions and engaging conversations. Your mind becomes more active and adaptable, craving mental stimulation and variety. This transit encourages you to explore different perspectives and gather information from various sources. You may feel a greater need to express your thoughts and feelings, seeking connections through meaningful dialogue.

11 Saturday

Essential changes offer blessings that feed inspiration and fuel your desire to adapt and grow. You set off on a new adventure that sets an exciting tone for increasing your world. A richly creative process is at the crux of this enterprising time. It draws a gentle element that beautifully accents your current lifestyle. A bright and breezy environment offers a radiant aspect that illuminates new possibilities. It gives your life a reboot and takes you to a happy chapter ahead.

12 Sunday

With Mars forming a trine aspect with Neptune, a harmonious blend of passion and imagination enhances your ability to pursue your dreams and creative endeavors with confidence and a touch of magic. You are motivated to take inspired action and manifest your visions into reality. Trust in your intuition and use this harmonious energy to tap into your artistic abilities, engage in spiritual practices, and channel your feelings into productive and meaningful pursuits.

13 Monday

With the Sun forming a trine with Uranus and a Full Moon illuminating the sky, you are entering a phase of exciting breakthroughs, unexpected changes, and heightened awareness. The Sun trine Uranus aspect sparks a sense of individuality and freedom within you. You can express your unique self and embrace your authenticity. This harmonious alignment encourages you to break free from old patterns and embrace new ideas and opportunities that come your way.

14 Tuesday

With the Moon entering Leo and Venus forming a square aspect with Jupiter, you are entering a period of heightened passion, creativity, and desire for joy and abundance. The Moon in Leo amplifies emotional expression and encourages you to embrace your inner light. You may crave attention, recognition, and love, seeking opportunities to radiate your authentic self. Meanwhile, Venus square Jupiter adds an element of indulgence and extravagance to your experiences.

15 Wednesday

In the eighth house, Mars in Cancer directs its transformative and intense energy towards matters of shared resources, intimacy, and the occult. Your approach to joint finances and deep connections is marked by emotional depth and a desire for security. You may excel in roles that involve investigating and transforming hidden truths, such as psychology or research. Your ability to channel your emotional energy into transformative processes can lead to profound growth.

16 Thursday

Embracing a diligent and analytical mindset will help you navigate the potential challenges of the Sun-Mars opposition and find practical solutions to any conflicts. Use this period to refine your plans, streamline your routines, and focus on the small but essential details contributing to your overall success. By harnessing the energy of the Virgo Moon, you can navigate any obstacles with precision and emerge with a sense of accomplishment and productivity.

17 Friday

With the Sun sextile Neptune, you may experience a harmonious blend of imagination and intuition. This aspect invites you to tap into your creative and spiritual potential, allowing inspiration to flow effortlessly. Your sense of empathy and compassion heightens, enabling you to connect deeply with others on an emotional level. You may attract artistic pursuits or spiritual practices that uplift and inspire you.

18 Saturday

Your willingness to open your life to meeting new people brings rising prospects into your social life. Sharing time with your circle of friends holds an essential key to growing your life outwardly. It jumpstarts an active time of developing meaningful bonds in your life. It lays the groundwork for connecting with your community and engaging in a group environment that helps you thrive and prosper.

19 Sunday

As Venus conjuncts Saturn, you may experience a blend of stability and seriousness in your relationships and personal values. This aspect brings a sense of commitment and responsibility to your interactions, urging you to approach matters of the heart with a grounded and practical mindset. With the Moon's ingress into Libra, your emotional focus turns towards seeking harmony and balance in your connections with others.

20 Monday

In the nurturing fourth house, Venus in Pisces influences your approach to home, family, and emotional security. You have a deep appreciation for creating a harmonious and aesthetically pleasing home environment. Your nurturing and empathetic nature contributes to a loving atmosphere within your family. Relationships with family members are often marked by emotional closeness and a desire to provide support and comfort.

21 Tuesday

As the Moon ingresses Scorpio, emotions intensify, and you may find yourself drawn to exploring the depths of your feelings. This aspect is a time of emotional transformation, where you can uncover profound insights and regenerate emotionally. It is an opportunity to release what no longer serves you and embrace emotional authenticity. It offers a potent blend of personal power, emotional depth, and the potential for profound change.

22 Wednesday

In the second house, Mercury in Capricorn influences your thought processes and communication style in matters of finance, values, and self-worth. Your practical and realistic approach to money matters is reflected in your financial decisions and communication about material possessions. You may excel in organizing and managing your resources efficiently. Strive for flexibility while still maintaining a practical mindset in your financial pursuits.

23 Thursday

With Mars sextile Uranus, you may experience the energy and a desire for change and innovation. This aspect brings a sense of excitement and the courage to break free from routine and embrace new possibilities. It encourages you to take bold and spontaneous actions, trust your instincts, and seek new experiences. Meanwhile, Mercury opposing Mars can bring tension and conflict in communication.

24 Friday

With the Moon's ingress into Sagittarius, you may feel a sense of expansion and a yearning for adventure in your emotional landscape. This aspect brings enthusiasm and optimism, encouraging you to explore new horizons and broaden your perspective. You may seek experiences that ignite your wanderlust and push your comfort zone's boundaries. Embrace the freedom to explore and seek knowledge and wisdom from different sources.

25 Saturday

With Venus trine Mars, a harmonious blend of passion, desire, and affection permeates your interactions and relationships. This aspect brings a harmonizing energy that allows you to express your wishes and pursue your passions. You feel a natural flow of attraction and magnetism, enhancing your personal and romantic connections. It's a time of increased confidence and assertiveness in pursuing what you want, whether in love, creativity, or personal goals.

26 Sunday

The Venus sextile Uranus aspect adds a touch of excitement and unpredictability to your relationships and social interactions. It brings opportunities for spontaneous connections and unique experiences. Your love life may take a surprising turn, and you may find yourself drawn to unconventional partnerships or exploring new avenues of self-expression. This aspect invites you to embrace change and welcome the unexpected in matters of the heart.

27 Monday

With the Sun in Aquarius gracing your third house, your intellectual and unconventional nature finds expression in communication, learning, and short journeys. You approach information with a unique and progressive mindset, often seeking knowledge that challenges traditional perspectives. Your communication style is marked by originality and a desire to promote innovation. You may find joy in collaborative intellectual pursuits that contribute to the greater good.

28 Tuesday

As the Moon ingresses Aquarius, your emotions align with the energy of progressiveness and humanitarian ideals. You may feel a strong sense of community and a desire to connect with like-minded individuals who share your values and vision for the future. This lunar placement promotes an understanding of emotional detachment and objectivity, allowing you to view situations from a broader perspective.

29 Wednesday

As the New Moon represents a fresh start, it is a powerful time to set personal growth and transformation intentions. Take advantage of this celestial alignment to delve into deep self-reflection, uncover hidden truths, and communicate your desires and aspirations with passion and determination. Embrace the transformative energy of Mercury conjunct Pluto and the rebirth potential of the New Moon as you embark on a journey of empowerment and profound change.

30 Thursday

The Sun trine Jupiter adds expansive and positive energy to your life. This alignment brings opportunities for growth, abundance, and optimism. You may feel renewed confidence and enthusiasm, allowing you to pursue your goals and aspirations. This aspect is a time to broaden your horizons, take risks, and embrace new experiences. Trust in the abundance of the universe and allow yourself to shine brightly.

FEBRUARY

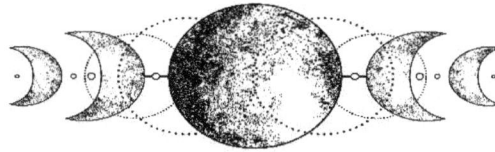

MOON MAGIC

Sun	Mon	Tue	Wed	Thu	Fri	Sat
						1
2	3	4	5	6	7	8
9	10	11	12	13	14	15
16	17	18	19	20	21	22
23	24	25	26	27	28	

NEW MOON

SNOW MOON

31 Friday

You soon link up with kindred spirits who promote collaborative opportunities. You discover a group environment that helps you design goals and plan ambitious projects. Trailblazing options bring brainstorming sessions that encourage inspiration and creativity. Advancement is brewing in the background and soon opens the path forward. Your willingness to deepen your knowledge focuses on learning unique areas that come calling.

1 Saturday

Today's alignment encourages you to embrace compassion, empathy, and unconditional love. It's a time to let your heart guide you, to infuse your relationships and experiences with a sense of magic and grace. Open yourself to the beauty surrounding you, and let the whispers of Venus and Neptune awaken your soul's longing for harmony and spiritual connection. This cosmic dance between Venus and Neptune encourages you to tap into your heart's desires.

2 Sunday

The Aries Moon empowers you to take charge of your life, make decisive choices, and enthusiastically go after what you want. Trust your instincts and allow your inner fire to guide you toward exciting adventures and self-discovery. Embrace the spirit of spontaneity and embrace the thrill of stepping outside your comfort zone. Let the energy of Aries fuel your passions and propel you toward personal growth and fulfillment.

3 Monday

Mercury trine Jupiter is an ideal time for learning, studying, or engaging in intellectual pursuits that broaden your horizons. You may find yourself drawn to philosophical or spiritual subjects, seeking wisdom and understanding. Embrace the opportunities that come your way, as this alignment supports growth, success, and abundant possibilities. Trust in your abilities and let your mind soar to new heights.

4 Tuesday

As the Moon moves into Taurus, you experience a sense of grounding and stability, settling into your emotions and inner world. Your focus shifts towards finding comfort and security in your surroundings, and you may feel a stronger connection to the physical aspects of life. Simultaneously, with Venus entering Aries, you feel a surge of passion and assertiveness in your relationships and creative endeavors. Your desires become more direct as you pursue areas of joy.

5 Wednesday

Syncing with the overhead cosmic energies primes you for a purposeful day, and there's a subtle suggestion of alignment and intention in the celestial forecast. The cosmic interplay invites you to harmonize with the vibrations surrounding your daily endeavors. Navigate your day with a purposeful dance of heavenly forces, allowing their rhythmic touch to guide you toward moments of focused execution and meaningful progress.

6 Thursday

As the Moon enters Gemini, a sense of curiosity and mental agility sweeps over you. The energy of Gemini encourages versatility and adaptability, allowing you to embrace change and explore different options. It's an excellent time to express your ideas and thoughts, as your words carry impact and influence. Harness the power of this lunar phase to engage in learning, connect with others, and let your curiosity guide you toward new horizons.

7 Friday

With Venus forming a sextile aspect to Pluto, transformative energy permeates your relationships and desires. You draw deeper connections and experiences that profoundly impact your emotional well-being. This aspect ignites passionate and intense fuel within you, encouraging you to explore your desires and pursue what resonates with your soul. You are empowered to let go of old patterns and embrace a more authentic and fulfilling expression of love and intimacy.

8 Saturday

Moon ingress Cancer. Trust your instincts and allow yourself to reveal the wisdom of your feelings. Connect with loved ones more deeply, offering support and understanding. Use this lunar energy to cultivate a sense of home and belonging within yourself and your relationships. Embrace the nurturing power of Cancer and allow it to nourish your soul, bringing you a greater understanding of emotional well-being.

9 Sunday

With the Sun and Mercury coming together in a powerful conjunction, your mind is sharp, and your communication skills heighten. This alignment brings clarity and focus to your thoughts, enabling you to express yourself with confidence and precision. You can articulate your ideas effectively and make a lasting impact through your words. Simultaneously, the harmonious trine between Mars and Saturn provides a grounded and disciplined approach to achieving your goals.

10 Monday

As the Moon enters Leo, your emotions amplify with a fiery passion. You are ready to shine and express yourself with confidence and enthusiasm. This energy encourages you to embrace your inner creativity and let your unique talents take center stage. You crave attention and recognition, seeking opportunities to showcase your individuality and leadership qualities. The Leo influence ignites your self-expression, inspiring you to share your joy and warmth with others.

11 Tuesday

When the Sun forms a square with Uranus, you may experience a period of unpredictability and change in your life. This aspect creates a sense of restlessness and a desire for freedom and individuality. You may crave new experiences and break free from routines or limitations. It's a time to embrace your unique quirks and the unconventional aspects of your personality. However, it's essential to approach this energy with caution, as it can also bring unexpected disruptions.

12 Wednesday

During a Full Moon, you may experience a sense of culmination or completion in various areas of your life. This lunar phase lets you gain clarity and insight into your emotions, relationships, and goals. It's a time of reflection and release, where you can let go of what no longer serves you and make space for new beginnings. The Full Moon brings a sense of intensity and energy, urging you to express yourself authentically and embrace your inner desires and passions.

13 Thursday

The Moon in Virgo encourages you to pay attention to your physical and mental well-being as you recognize the importance of taking care of yourself on all levels. Use this time to create a harmonious environment and establish healthy habits that support your overall productivity and success. Embrace the Earthy energy of Virgo to bring order and structure into your life, helping you to thrive in both your personal and professional endeavors.

14 Friday

As Mercury moves into Pisces, you are attuned to emotions, compassion, and romantic connections. Your communication style may become more intuitive, poetic, and empathetic, allowing you to express your feelings with depth and sensitivity. It is a time to connect on a soulful level, as your words carry a certain magic that can touch the hearts of others. You may daydream and tap into your imagination, allowing for creative and romantic expressions.

15 Saturday

As the Moon moves into Libra, you may feel a sense of harmony and a desire for balance. This transit focuses on relationships and partnerships, encouraging you to seek unity and cooperation. You may find yourself more attuned to the needs and perspectives of those around you, fostering a sense of empathy and understanding. It's an excellent time to engage in social activities, connect with loved ones, and cultivate a peaceful and harmonious atmosphere.

16 Sunday

Taking a moment to balance your energies brings rising prospects for a harmonious day; there's a subtle suggestion of equilibrium and ease in the celestial forecast. The cosmic interplay invites you to find balance within the vibrations surrounding your daily tasks. Navigate your day with a fluid dance of heavenly forces, allowing their gentle touch to guide you toward moments of smooth execution and natural progression.

17 Monday

You are ready to open the floodgates and embrace a brighter chapter. Being open to growing your circle of friends lets you adopt a journey that captures the essence of inspiration. It brings a more social environment that tempts you out and about. Engaging with a broader world of potential brings a refreshing change of pace to your life. An invitation to mingle ahead carries you forward on the winds of change.

18 Tuesday

Moon ingress Scorpio. Sun ingress Pisces. Your intuition and imagination amplify, allowing you to tap into the subtle nuances of your surroundings. It's a period of heightened sensitivity where you may find solace in artistic or spiritual pursuits. Embrace this harmonious blend of Scorpio's depth and Pisces' compassion, allowing it to guide you on a journey of self-discovery as you revel in the transformative and transcendent energies these transits bring forth.

19 Wednesday

As you become immersed in the cosmic rhythm of your daily grind, subtle energies beckon you to infuse your tasks with determination and resolve. The celestial dance invites you to immerse yourself in the dynamic vibrations that surround your daily agenda. Embrace the harmonious dance of cosmic forces within your routines, allowing their invigorating touch to guide you toward moments of accomplishment and focused determination.

20 Thursday

Moon ingress Sagittarius. Mercury Square Jupiter. Take the time to analyze information carefully and consider the potential consequences before making important decisions. This aspect challenges you to balance your desire for expansion and the need for realistic thinking. By harnessing the Sagittarian spirit of exploration while maintaining a practical mindset, you can navigate this period with wisdom and make the most of the opportunities that come your way.

21 Friday

Celestial configurations hint at subtle shifts and opportune potential in your daily landscape. These cosmic whispers suggest a narrative of luck and favorable circumstances throughout your day. The celestial dance invites you to immerse yourself in the rhythmic vibrations that surround your daily agenda. Engage with the hints presented by the stellar configurations, allowing their guidance to enhance your connection with the cosmic energies that shape your daily plans.

22 Saturday

As the Moon enters Capricorn, you move with determination and practicality. Capricorn's influence encourages you to focus on your goals, take charge of your responsibilities, and approach tasks with discipline and structure. It's a time to prioritize your ambitions and work diligently towards achieving them. The grounded energy of Capricorn helps you stay focused and committed, even when faced with challenges or setbacks.

23 Sunday

With the Sun illuminating your fourth house, the Pisces energy takes on a more nurturing and empathetic quality in matters of home, family, and emotional security. You approach domestic life with a compassionate and intuitive mindset, often seeking to create a harmonious and serene environment. Your connection to your roots and family may be deeply spiritual, and you find solace in activities that allow you to tap into your emotional and imaginative depths.

24 Monday

Mars turns direct, which is a time to channel your passion and enthusiasm into concrete actions, make bold moves, and embrace opportunities for growth and achievement. With Mars' forward energy fueling your endeavors, you can make significant strides and experience renewed momentum in your personal and professional pursuits. Trust your inner fire and let it propel you toward fulfilling your dreams.

25 Tuesday

As the Moon enters Aquarius, you may experience a heightened sense of individuality and intellectual curiosity. This lunar influence encourages you to embrace your unique perspective and seek unconventional ways of thinking. Simultaneously, the conjunction between Mercury and Saturn brings focused and disciplined energy to communication and thought processes. It's a time when your words carry weight, and careful planning and attention to detail lead to success.

26 Wednesday

Within the harmonious cosmic frequencies for an intentional day, there's a suggestion of purpose and practicality in the air. This cosmic alignment encourages a rhythmic flow of purposeful activities and a steady sense of direction. Embrace the nuanced interplay of celestial forces within your daily routine, navigating your tasks with a heightened awareness of the harmonious dance orchestrating the cosmic symphony throughout your workday.

27 Thursday

Mars in Cancer brings a passionate and emotionally charged energy to the cosmic exploration of the eighth house. Feel the assertive undercurrents as Mars encourages you to confront and transform emotional challenges with vigor and intensity. Under this celestial influence, delve fearlessly into the mysteries of intimate connections, using Mars' assertiveness to navigate the complexities of transformative experiences with emotional strength and resilience.

MARCH

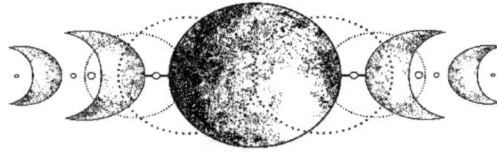

MOON MAGIC

Sun	Mon	Tue	Wed	Thu	Fri	Sat
						1
2	3	4	5	6	7	8
9	10	11	12	13	14	15
16	17	18	19	20	21	22
23	24	25	26	27	28	29
30	31					

NEW MOON

WORM MOON

_____

_____

_____

_____

_____

_____

_____

_____

_____

_____

_____

_____

_____

_____

_____

_____

_____

_____

_____

_____

_____

28 Friday

During the New Moon phase, you have an opportunity for fresh beginnings and setting intentions for the future. This lunar cycle invites you to reflect on your goals, desires, and aspirations. It is a time of initiation and planting seeds for growth. You can take this moment to envision what you want to manifest in your life and align your actions with your intentions. The New Moon symbolizes a blank canvas where you can start anew and create your desired life.

1 Saturday

The Aries energy ignites your inner spark, encouraging you to embrace individuality and assert your desires. You draw new beginnings and are eager to chase after your goals. Use this dynamic energy to fuel your passions and take decisive action. Trust your instincts and embrace the spirit of bravery as you step with a renewed sense of purpose and determination. Let the Moon in Aries inspire you to embrace your inner warrior and fearlessly pursue.

2 Sunday

As Venus turns retrograde, it invites introspection and reevaluation of your relationships and values. It is a time to reflect on matters of the heart, explore your desires, and examine the foundations of your connections. With Mercury conjunct Neptune, your intuition and imagination heighten, offering you a deeper understanding of your emotions and the unseen realms. It's a time to trust your inner voice and pay attention to subtle cues in your interactions.

3 Monday

With Mercury's ingress into Aries, your thoughts and communication style take on a more direct and assertive tone. You feel a surge of mental energy and a desire to take action on your ideas and plans. Speak your mind with confidence and courage, expressing your opinions and asserting your needs. Meanwhile, the Moon's ingress into Taurus brings a sense of groundedness to your emotions. You seek security in familiar surroundings and may find solace in simple pleasures.

4 Tuesday

Celestial configurations hint at subtle shifts and transformative potential in your daily landscape. These cosmic whispers suggest a narrative of growth and evolution throughout your day. Engage with the hints presented by the celestial configurations, allowing their guidance to enhance your understanding of the cosmic energies that shape your daily plans. The astrological landscape invites you to dance with the divine threads that shape your daily narrative.

5 Wednesday

As the Moon enters Gemini, you seek intellectual stimulation. Your mind becomes sharper and more adaptable, allowing you to absorb information quickly and engage in lively conversations. Your social interactions become more dynamic, and you find joy in connecting with others through meaningful dialogue. With Mercury sextile Pluto, your mental faculties enhance, and you possess a profound insight into the hidden depths of situations.

6 Thursday

The celestial signatures inscribed in the cosmic canvas suggest a story of dynamism and cosmic nuances within your personal experiences. Embrace the unfolding tale written in the heavenly language, allowing the astrological landscape to guide your interpretations and actions throughout your day, inviting you to dance harmoniously with the celestial threads that shape your daily narrative across various aspects of your life.

7 Friday

You may feel more attuned to the needs of your loved ones, offering them emotional support and a listening ear. It's a time to honor and express your feelings, allowing yourself to be vulnerable and seeking solace in the nurturing energy of the home. You seek comfort in familiar spaces and engage in activities that provide emotional nourishment. Trust your instincts and prioritize self-care as you navigate the ebb and flow of emotions during this Moon in Cancer transit.

8 Saturday

Sun trine Mars. You may find yourself more proactive and courageous in pursuing your passions and asserting yourself in various areas of your life. It's important to channel this energy constructively, focusing on productive endeavors and maintaining a balanced approach. Embrace the opportunities that arise, trust your abilities, and take bold steps toward your aspirations. The Sun trines Mars and invites you to seize the day and maximize your potential.

9 Sunday

As the Moon enters Leo, you discover rising self-expression and creativity. Your emotions take on a vibrant and dramatic quality, fueling your desire to shine. This lunar transit encourages you to embrace and share your inner radiance with the world. You feel a strong pull to engage in activities that bring you joy and allow your unique personality to take center stage. It's a time to let your light shine brightly to express your passions and talents confidently.

10 Monday

Celestial configurations hint at subtle shifts and opportune potential in your workday landscape. These cosmic whispers suggest a narrative of productivity and favorable circumstances throughout your professional endeavors. Engage with the hints presented by the celestial configurations, allowing their guidance to enhance your understanding and connection with the cosmic energies that shape your workday plans.

11 Tuesday

When Mercury and Venus align, it brings a harmonious blending of intellect and romance into your life. This celestial combination enhances your ability to express yourself with grace, charm, and diplomacy. Your communication style becomes more refined, and you find it easier to convey your thoughts and feelings pleasingly and persuasively. Your words are sweet, and your interactions fill with warmth and harmony.

12 Wednesday

Moon ingress Virgo. Sun conjunct Saturn. You may need self-discipline and be inclined to take a more serious and measured approach to your tasks and responsibilities. Embrace the productive energy available, prioritize your obligations, and stay committed to your objectives. By embracing the qualities of diligence and perseverance, you can make significant progress and lay the groundwork for your success.

13 Thursday

Within the harmonious cosmic frequencies for a balanced daily routine, there's a suggestion of adaptability and practicality in the air. This cosmic alignment encourages a rhythmic flow of flexible activities and a responsive approach to your daily tasks. Embrace the nuanced interplay of celestial forces within your routine, navigating your day with a heightened awareness of the harmonious dance orchestrating the cosmic symphony in your daily life.

14 Friday

The Sun's sextile with Uranus brings opportunities for unexpected breakthroughs and innovative thinking. You may feel a surge of creative energy and a willingness to step outside your comfort zone to explore new possibilities. With the Moon entering Libra, there is a focus on diplomacy, compromise, and seeking harmony in your interactions with others. You can use this energy to build stronger relationships and create a more balanced and peaceful environment.

15 Saturday

While Mercury retrograde may bring challenges and delays, it offers valuable lessons and insights. Embrace this period as an opportunity for self-discovery, inner growth, and refining your approach to communication. By taking a step back, reviewing your choices, and making necessary adjustments, you can navigate this retrograde phase with greater awareness and emerge stronger and wiser on the other side.

16 Sunday

As you become immersed in the cosmic flow of your daily home life, subtle energies beckon you to infuse your domestic activities with fluidity and purpose. The celestial dance invites you to immerse yourself in the rhythmic vibrations that surround your home routines. Embrace the harmonious dance of cosmic forces within your personal space, allowing their flowing touch to guide you toward moments of comfort and tranquility.

17 Monday

When the Moon ingresses Scorpio, you may feel a deep emotional intensity and a desire to delve into the depths of your feelings. It is a time of heightened sensitivity and introspection, where you can explore your innermost desires and uncover hidden truths. You may find yourself experiencing powerful emotions and a strong need for intimacy and connection. Use this time to self-reflect, allowing yourself to face unresolved issues or buried emotions.

18 Tuesday

With Uranus in Taurus gracing your sixth house of daily routines and work, the cosmic disruptor introduces a paradigm shift in your approach to responsibilities. Feel the revolutionary energy as Uranus encourages you to break free from monotonous patterns and embrace innovative methods in your daily tasks. Under this celestial influence, your work environment becomes a dynamic space for experimentation and cutting-edge solutions.

19 Wednesday

As the Moon enters Sagittarius, it brings a sense of expansion and adventure to your emotional experiences. You may feel a renewed optimism and enthusiasm for life as the energy of Sagittarius encourages you to explore new horizons and embrace the unknown. With the Sun conjunct with Neptune, there is dreaminess and idealism around you. This alignment invites you to tap into your imagination and connect with your intuition on a deeper level.

20 Thursday

Sun ingress Aries. Vernal Equinox. The Equinox symbolizes a balance between light and darkness, reminding you to find harmony within yourself and your surroundings. It's a time to set intentions, plant growth seeds, and embrace life's natural cycles. Allow the energy of Aries and Equinox to propel you forward, empowering you to embrace your true potential and embark on a journey of self-expression and personal fulfillment.

21 Friday

The sextile between Venus and Pluto offers a potent blend of magnetism and emotional depth, enabling you to attract and foster meaningful relationships that have the potential to transform your life. It's a time to embrace your power and harness the transformative energy available, fostering deep connections that bring pleasure and growth. Open your heart and allow the magic of this alignment to guide profound and transformative experiences in love and relationships.

22 Saturday

When the Moon ingresses Capricorn, you may notice a shift towards a more grounded and disciplined emotional state. Capricorn energy brings a sense of practicality, responsibility, and ambition to your emotions. You may focus more on long-term goals and work diligently to achieve them. This transit encourages you to take a structured and organized approach to your feelings, seeking stability and control.

23 Sunday

Sun conjunct Venus. Sun sextile Pluto. It is a time of heightened self-confidence as you radiate magnetic energy that attracts positive opportunities and deep connections. Embrace the transformative potential of this alignment by embracing your passions, nurturing your relationships, and tapping into your inner strength to create positive change in your life. Allow the powerful energy of the Sun and Pluto to empower you on your journey of self-discovery and growth.

24 Monday

Moon ingress Aquarius. Sun conjunct Mercury. This energy encourages you to embrace individuality, think outside the box, and explore new perspectives. It is perfect for brainstorming, problem-solving, and seeking intellectual stimulation. You may be attracted to academic pursuits, social causes, and collaborative endeavors promoting positive change. Embrace this period of mental acuity and let your ideas flow as you connect with others on a deeper level.

25 Tuesday

When Mercury sextiles Pluto, you may experience a profound depth of thought and an increased ability to delve into the depths of your mind. This aspect enhances your analytical and investigative skills, allowing you to uncover hidden truths and gain deeper insights into various subjects. Your communication style may become more intense and persuasive as you possess a natural knack for finding conversations' underlying motives and dynamics.

26 Wednesday

When the Moon enters Pisces, you may feel a gentle shift in your emotional landscape. Your sensitivity heightens, and you are more attuned to the subtle energies around you. It's a time to embrace your compassionate nature and extend kindness and understanding to others. You may find solace in creative pursuits, immersing yourself in art, music, or writing. Your strong intuition guides you to trust your inner voice and follow your heart's desires.

27 Thursday

When the Black Moon enters Scorpio, and Venus moves into Pisces, you may experience transformative energy in love, relationships, and self-expression. Embark on a journey of self-discovery and personal transformation. The Black Moon's intense and mysterious Scorpio energy invites you to delve into your emotions and confront any hidden desires or fears holding you back. It's a time for exploring your shadow and embracing transformation's power.

28 Friday

As the Moon enters Aries, you feel a surge of fiery and dynamic energy within you. It's a time of initiation and new beginnings, where your passions and ambitions reignite. You may feel a sense of enthusiasm and courage, ready to take on challenges and assert yourself in various areas of your life. This lunar transit inspires you to embrace individuality and confidently assert your needs and desires.

29 Saturday

During the New Moon phase, you reveal a fresh start and a blank canvas to create your future. It's a time of new beginnings and setting intentions. You can plant the seeds of your desires and watch them grow throughout the lunar cycle by envisioning what you want to manifest in your life. Use this time to connect with your inner wisdom and align with your true desires. Trust the process and believe in your ability to create the life you envision.

30 Sunday

As Mercury enters Pisces and aligns with Neptune, imagination and intuition heighten. Your mind becomes a gateway to ethereal realms where creativity and spiritual insights flow freely. With Neptune transitioning into Aries, you embark on a journey of self-discovery and assertiveness. This celestial shift empowers you to embrace individuality and express your unique voice. As the Moon enters Taurus, grounding and stability become your allies, providing a solid foundation.

APRIL

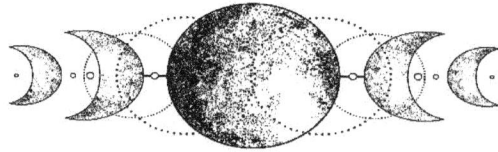

MOON MAGIC

Sun	Mon	Tue	Wed	Thu	Fri	Sat
		1	2	3	4	5
6	7	8	9	10	11	12
13	14	15	16	17	18	19
20	21	22	23	24	25	26
27	28	29	30			

NEW MOON

PINK MOON

31 Monday

A shift forward brings a lovely boost to your world. It does highlight new options that encourage you to expand your horizons. You can create abundance by exploring all that life has to offer. A further possibility emerges that causes a great deal of excitement. It revolves around learning a new area, which creates a productive growth phase. You generate your leads and can go for gold. Fortune lights a shimmering path that makes you eager to begin a new journey.

1 Tuesday

As the Moon enters Gemini, you may feel a shift in your mental energy and a heightened curiosity. This transit encourages you to embrace versatility, adaptability, and intellectual stimulation. Your mind becomes agile and nimble, ready to explore new ideas, engage in lively conversations, and gather information from various sources. It's a time to embrace your natural curiosity, express your thoughts and concepts, and connect with others intellectually.

2 Wednesday

Within the realm of creativity and self-expression, the Sun in Aries sparks a cosmic fire, infusing your artistic pursuits and romantic endeavors with passion and vitality. Your approach to love becomes bold and adventurous, embracing the thrill of romantic pursuits and creative self-expression. The Sun encourages you to shine brightly in matters of the heart, expressing your authentic self with courage and assertiveness.

3 Thursday

As the Moon transitions into Cancer, you may find yourself experiencing heightened emotions and a deep longing for security and nurturing. Your intuition becomes more prominent, guiding you to listen to your inner voice and honor your feelings. You can welcome the positive changes that come your way. During this lunar phase, you may desire to create a sense of home and comfort in your surroundings, seeking solace and support from loved ones.

4 Friday

Saturn sextile Uranus. Mars sextile Uranus. You can navigate challenges and obstacles with resilience and determination, finding creative solutions that blend the old and the new. Embrace the synergy of these sextile aspects as they support you in manifesting your dreams and bringing positive transformations into your life. Trust in your ability to find the perfect balance between stability and change; you will navigate this dynamic energy with grace and success.

5 Saturday

When Mars forms a trine with Saturn, it brings a harmonious blend of energy and discipline into your life. You can channel your ambitions and desires into practical actions and long-term goals. This aspect supports building a solid foundation and working diligently towards your aspirations. You possess the stamina and perseverance to overcome obstacles and setbacks and the strategic thinking to plan your steps carefully.

6 Sunday

Today, the planetary configuration fosters a harmonious balance between your personal needs and the needs of others, supporting collaborative efforts and positive connections. You are encouraged to express your authentic self, radiate warmth and generosity, and embrace the joy of living with an open heart. Let the Moon in Leo, the Sun sextile Jupiter, and the Venus trine Mars inspire you to shine brightly, expand your horizons, and create meaningful connections.

7 Monday

As Mercury turns direct, you can expect a shift in communication and mental clarity. After introspection and reflection during its retrograde phase, Mercury moves forward, allowing you to express yourself more freely and confidently and make decisions. Any previous misunderstandings or delays may begin to untangle, and you'll find it easier to move forward with plans, projects, and essential conversations.

8 Tuesday

With Venus's harmonious sextile aspect to Uranus, you may experience exciting and unexpected relationships and personal values shifts. This alignment brings a sense of excitement, novelty, and freedom to your interactions and the way you approach love. You may be attracted to unconventional, unique individuals or situations challenging the status quo. It's a time to embrace individuality and express your authentic self in your relationships and creative pursuits.

9 Wednesday

With Neptune in your sixth house, the cosmic currents of inspiration gently permeate the realm of work and daily routines. Feel the ethereal energies infusing your tasks with a touch of enchantment, inviting you to approach your responsibilities with a creative and intuitive mindset. Under the celestial guidance, let your work become a cosmic dance, blending practicality with artistic flair. Neptune guides you toward a harmonious fusion of productivity and inspiration.

10 Thursday

In the domain of partnerships and relationships, Jupiter in Gemini brings a spirit of intellectual exploration and communicative expansiveness. Feel the cosmic currents of expansion flowing through your connections, fostering a lively exchange of ideas and a shared love for learning. Under this celestial influence, relationships become a dynamic playground for intellectual growth, where mutual curiosity and open-minded communication create an enriching cosmic dance.

APRIL

11 Friday

With the Moon's ingress into Libra, you may feel a heightened sense of harmony, balance, and a desire for peace in your interactions and surroundings. This lunar influence encourages you to seek fairness and cooperation in your relationships, valuing compromise and diplomacy. You may find yourself more attuned to the needs and perspectives of others, fostering a cooperative and harmonious atmosphere in your social connections.

12 Saturday

News ahead carries new possibilities that draw a lighter chapter into your life. Things are on the move soon as your focus shifts towards developing your talents as you unleash your abilities in an active environment that offers progression. An influx of information brings new options into your life, helping you move progressively and sustainably toward developing unique goals. Tweaking goals and mapping out your plan brings insight into the path ahead.

13 Sunday

As the Moon transitions into Scorpio, you may dive deeper into your emotional depths, explore hidden desires, and seek transformation. This ingress is a powerful time to self-reflect, uncover your innermost truths, and embrace the potential for personal growth. Be open to the transformative energies of Scorpio and use this period to release any emotional burdens and step into a renewed sense of authenticity and empowerment.

14 Monday

News arrives that offers an exciting change. A snap decision cracks the code to a vibrant landscape. Life picks up steam, bringing new flavors and possibilities that inspire growth. Broadening horizons offers room to grow a path that sees potential blossoming. Being open to new leads encourages creative thinking. It lets you come up with a winning destination. It offers an enterprising approach that develops new goals.

15 Tuesday

Resources and support help you get busy manifesting your vision. Information that allows progress on your path forward arrives soon. It brings the right time to begin working on your career goals. It enables you to build remarkable growth and prosperity; changes ahead extend your reach into a new area of possibility. It offers a carefree time that heightens creativity and brings new projects and assignments worthy of your attention.

16 Wednesday

As the Moon ingresses into Sagittarius, a sense of adventure and expansiveness fills the air, inspiring you to seek new horizons and broaden your perspective. It's a time to embrace spontaneity, explore different cultures, and expand your knowledge through learning and travel. Simultaneously, Mercury's ingress into Aries makes your communication style more assertive and direct. You feel a surge of mental energy, empowering you to express your thoughts confidently.

17 Thursday

Mercury conjunct Neptune. Your communication style may take on a poetic or imaginative tone as you express yourself in ways beyond logic and rationality. It's a time to tap into your creative potential, explore the mysteries of the universe, and engage in deep, soulful conversations. Embrace the ethereal energy of Mercury conjunct Neptune, and allow yourself to feel inspired by the hidden depths of your imagination.

18 Friday

As Mars enters Leo and the Moon moves into Capricorn, you may experience a dynamic combination of passion, drive, and a strong sense of responsibility. Mars in Leo ignites your inner fire, urging you to express yourself confidently. You feel motivated to pursue goals with vigor and enthusiasm, fueled by a desire for recognition and success. The Moon in Capricorn adds a grounding influence, reminding you to approach ambitions with discipline and a long-term perspective.

19 Saturday

As the Sun gracefully enters Taurus, it brings a sense of stability and groundedness to your life. This energy encourages you to embrace the pleasures of the physical world and find comfort in the simplicity of everyday experiences. Slow down, savor the present moment, and cultivate a deeper connection with your senses. At the same time, the harmonious trine between Mars and Neptune amplifies your creative and spiritual potential.

20 Sunday

On this Easter Sunday, a day filled with hope and new beginnings, you are greeted with celestial alignments that ignite a spark of excitement and transformation. Venus sextile Uranus invites unexpected encounters and delightful surprises into your life. Love and relationships take on an electrifying energy; simultaneously, Mercury sextile Pluto deepens your understanding and communication skills, empowering you to uncover truths and engage in meaningful conversations.

21 Monday

You may experience tension and friction as the Sun squares Mars during this period. This aspect brings a clash between your desires, ambitions, and the need for self-expression. It's essential to be mindful of impulsive reactions and the potential for conflicts to arise. Your energy and drive may heighten, but channeling them is crucial to avoid unnecessary conflicts or confrontations. Taking a step to assess situations helps you navigate this energy with grace.

22 Tuesday

Within the harmonious cosmic frequencies for a balanced daily routine, there's a suggestion of adaptability and practicality in the air. This cosmic alignment encourages a rhythmic flow of flexible activities and a responsive approach to your daily tasks. Embrace the nuanced interplay of celestial forces within your routine, navigating your day with a heightened awareness of the harmonious dance orchestrating the cosmic symphony in your daily life.

23 Wednesday

A breakthrough occurs regarding a dream that previously seemed out of reach. It hits the ticket for a productive time of developing life in a new direction. Projects crop up that inspire you and encourage the innovative use of your skills. Investigating options brings a cycle of growth that expands horizons. Breaking from limitations and extending your life brings unique adventures that reveal a journey that blossoms into a meaningful path forward.

24 Thursday

With the Sun gracing Taurus in your sixth house of daily routines and well-being, the cosmic luminary invites you to find joy in practical aspects of everyday life. The Sun encourages you to approach your work and health practices with a patient and methodical mindset, appreciating the tangible results of your efforts. Embrace the enduring qualities of Taurus as you create a harmonious and grounded routine, allowing the Sun to shine its gentle light on your well-being.

25 Friday

As Venus aligns with Saturn in conjunction, it brings a sense of responsibility and commitment to your relationships and values. You may find yourself more focused on long-term stability and practicality in matters of the heart. The Moon's ingress into Aries adds an assertive and energetic flair to your emotions, igniting a desire for independence and self-expression. This combination of energies encourages you to balance cravings and relationship stability.

26 Saturday

Celestial configurations hint at subtle shifts and opportune potential in your social interactions throughout the day. These cosmic whispers suggest a narrative of connection and enjoyable moments with friends or community. Engage with the hints presented by the celestial configurations, allowing their guidance to enhance your understanding and connection with the cosmic energies that shape your social life.

27 Sunday

When Mars opposes Pluto, you may feel a heightened intensity and power struggles within yourself and your interactions with others. This aspect can create a clash between your desires for control and transformation. It's essential to be mindful of power dynamics and avoid engaging in manipulative behaviors. Meanwhile, with the Moon entering Taurus and the arrival of a New Moon, there is an opportunity for new beginnings and grounding energy.

MAY

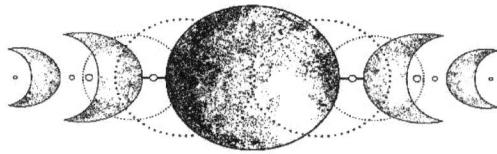

MOON MAGIC

Sun	Mon	Tue	Wed	Thu	Fri	Sat
				1	2	3
4	5	6	7	8	9	10
11	12	13	14	15	16	17
18	19	20	21	22	23	24
25	26	27	28	29	30	31

New Moon

FLOWER MOON

28 Monday

Aligning your energy with the cosmic energies promotes a harmonious day; there's a subtle suggestion of balance and focus in the celestial forecast. The cosmic interplay invites you to find equilibrium in your professional pursuits. Navigate your day with a graceful dance of heavenly forces, allowing their rhythmic touch to guide you towards moments of productivity and collaborative success in your work environment.

29 Tuesday

When the Moon enters Gemini, you may feel more curious, adaptable, and mentally stimulated. This planetary aspect is a time to embrace your versatility and engage in intellectual pursuits. Your mind becomes sharper, and you'll likely seek new experiences and gather information from various sources. Communication takes center stage, and you may feel more inclined to engage in conversations, express your thoughts, and connect with others mentally.

30 Wednesday

As Venus ingresses into Aries, it offers fiery passion and assertiveness in your relationships and personal desires. This transit brings independent energy to your interactions, inspiring you to follow what you want enthusiastically. Exciting and adventurous experiences result from taking bold initiatives in matters of the heart. Venus in Aries encourages you to express your individuality and assert your needs, embracing a more direct and proactive approach to love and relationships.

1 Thursday

As the Moon enters Cancer, you may notice a heightened emotional sensitivity and a deeper connection to your inner world. Cancer, ruled by the Moon, is a water sign known for its nurturing and compassionate energy. During this time, you might find yourself more attuned to your emotions and the needs of those around you. Your intuition and empathy heighten, allowing you to offer comfort and support to others.

MAY

2 Friday

You may experience a heightened sense of romance, imagination, and artistic inspiration when Venus and Neptune align. This celestial dance between the planet of love and beauty, Venus, and the world of dreams and spirituality, Neptune, invites you to explore the realms of fantasy and enchantment. You might find yourself captivated by the allure of beauty in all its forms, from art and music to nature and human connection.

3 Saturday

When the Moon enters Leo, you may feel vibrant energy and a desire to express your individuality. This astrological event encourages you to shine your light, embrace your unique talents, and share your creative essence with the world. You might find yourself seeking attention and recognition, as Leo is associated with self-confidence and the need for appreciation. Use this time to let your inner fire burn brightly and engage in activities that bring you joy and fulfillment.

4 Sunday

Pluto turns retrograde. This retrograde period encourages you to embrace your power and reclaim any aspects of yourself that have been buried or suppressed. It's a potent time for inner healing and rebirth as you release old patterns and make space for new growth and transformation. It's a time to release old baggage, heal emotional wounds, and emerge more empowered. Trust in the wisdom of this cosmic cycle, and allow yourself to discover the unseen forces at work within you.

5 Monday

When Mercury forms a sextile with Jupiter, you may experience optimism and intellectual expansion. This harmonious alignment between the planet of communication and the world of wisdom encourages you to broaden your horizons and seek knowledge. Your mind is sharp, and you are naturally curious to explore new ideas, philosophies, and perspectives. This aspect fosters positive thinking, effective communication, and the ability to articulate thoughts clearly.

6 Tuesday

When Venus forms a sextile aspect with Pluto, you may experience a deepening of your relationships and a heightened emotional intensity. This alignment fosters transformative experiences in love, passion, and intimacy. You may find yourself drawn to influential connections and have the ability to establish profound bonds with others. This energy encourages you to explore the depths of your emotions and embrace your desires with a sense of empowerment.

7 Wednesday

You become immersed in the cosmic flow of your daily work life; subtle energies beckon you to infuse your professional activities with fluidity and purpose. The celestial dance invites you to immerse yourself in the rhythmic vibrations that surround your work routines. Embrace the harmonious dance of cosmic forces within your work environment, allowing their flowing touch to guide you towards moments of accomplishment and inspired productivity.

8 Thursday

When the Moon moves into Libra, you may seek harmony and balance. You have a natural inclination towards fairness, diplomacy, and collaboration. Your focus turns towards creating harmonious relationships and finding common ground with others. This cosmic aspect is when you may feel more attuned to the needs and emotions of those around you, and you are likely to approach conflicts with a desire for compromise and understanding.

9 Friday

Venus in Aries sparks a cosmic fire, infusing your artistic pursuits with boldness and vitality. Your approach to love and romance becomes passionate and adventurous as the dynamic energy of Aries fuels your desires. Venus encourages you to embrace the thrill of romantic pursuits and creative endeavors. This celestial influence invites you to appreciate the beauty in assertive self-expression, whether through artistic projects or passionate connections.

10 Saturday

As Mercury moves into Taurus and the Moon enters Scorpio, you may experience a shift in your mental and emotional focus. With Mercury in Taurus, your thoughts become grounded and practical, and you may find yourself seeking stability and tangible results in your communication and decision-making processes. This transit encourages you to take time, think through, and approach situations deliberately and patiently.

11 Sunday

In the realm of daily routines and well-being, Mercury in Taurus influences your sixth house on Mother's Day, emphasizing the practical aspects of your relationship with your mother or mother figures. Conversations may center around health, routine care, and the simple pleasures that contribute to overall well-being. Mercury in Taurus encourages you to express gratitude through practical gestures, creating a serene environment that promotes relaxation.

MAY

12 Monday

Full Moon. Mercury square Pluto. It's essential to be mindful of your words and the potential for intense emotional reactions during this time. Utilize the transformative energy of the Full Moon to gain clarity and insight, but also be aware of the potential for confrontations or power dynamics in your communication. You can navigate this aspect with wisdom and self-awareness by staying grounded and open-minded.

13 Tuesday

The energy of Sagittarius Moon stimulates a thirst for knowledge and a desire to understand the world on a deeper level. It's a time to engage in meaningful conversations, embark on intellectual pursuits, and seek out opportunities for personal growth. Allow Sagittarius's fiery and enthusiastic energy to fuel your passions and inspire you to step outside your comfort zone. Embrace the spirit of adventure and let your curiosity guide you towards exciting possibilities.

14 Wednesday

As you create a bridge towards growing your dreams, you discover a venture that opens the door wide. A turning point occurs that offers advancement for your working life. It lets you dive into uncharted territory and find growth is possible when you push against the barriers of perceived expectations. An opportunity ahead fosters rising optimism. You get involved in learning an area that holds water and revs up the success rate for your career.

15 Thursday

The energy of Capricorn Moon encourages you to take a structured and organized approach to your tasks, allowing you to progress steadily toward your objectives. It's an excellent time to assess your ambitions, set realistic plans, and work diligently towards them. You may also need stability and security to establish a solid foundation for future endeavors. Embrace the influence of Capricorn and let it guide you in building a stable and fulfilling path ahead.

16 Friday

Life heads towards an upswing soon. It brings a social aspect that offers inspiring conversations. It marks a time of information and communication that lets you see the path ahead more clearly. Ideas flow as creativity heightens and provides a dynamic approach to developing new goals and projects. An area you get involved with planning receives the green light to move forward, bringing a stir of excitement into your world.

17 Saturday

When the Sun aligns with Uranus, you may experience a surge of energy and a desire for change and freedom. This powerful conjunction can bring unexpected events or opportunities that push you out of your comfort zone and into new territories. It's a time when you may feel inspired to break free from old patterns, embrace your uniqueness, and explore new possibilities. The Sun's radiant energy and Uranus' revolutionary influence can ignite a sense of innovation within you.

18 Sunday

When Mercury squares Mars, it can create tense and dynamic energy in your communication and mental processes. You may feel more assertive and inclined to speak your mind, but be cautious of impulsive or aggressive reactions that could lead to conflicts or misunderstandings. This aspect can bring about a clash between your thoughts and actions, making it essential to find a balance between being assertive and mindful of your words' impact on others.

19 Monday

Leaning into your strengths enables a pleasing result. The path ahead clears, bringing a succession of positive outcomes that have you feeling optimistic about your career life. Focusing on the building blocks and setting your intentions enables you to make the most of the changes ahead. As you deepen your knowledge and advance your skills, you extend your reach into new areas worth your time. A new phase soon cranks up the level of growth in your career.

20 Tuesday

As the Sun enters Gemini, it sparks a period of curiosity, adaptability, and intellectual stimulation. Your focus may shift toward learning, communication, and social interactions. It is a good time for networking, gathering information, and expressing thoughts. Embrace the versatility of Gemini energy and explore diverse interests and ideas. Balance your mental agility with the grounded wisdom of Saturn and the intuitive flow of Pisces to make the most of this dynamic energy.

21 Wednesday

As you synchronize with cosmic energies, you open a creatively charged day; there's a subtle suggestion of inspiration and innovation in the celestial forecast. The cosmic interplay invites you to align with your creative energies. Navigate your day with a vibrant dance of heavenly forces, allowing their dynamic touch to guide you toward moments of imaginative breakthroughs and self-expression in your creative endeavors.

22 Thursday

Venus forms a harmonious trine aspect with Mars, bringing a beautiful balance between passion and harmony in your relationships and endeavors. You may feel a surge of energy and confidence, allowing you to express your desires with grace and assertiveness. This aspect enhances your magnetism and attractiveness, attracting positive experiences and connections. With the Sun forming a sextile aspect with Neptune, your imagination and intuition rise.

23 Friday

Celestial configurations hint at subtle shifts and opportune potential in your workday landscape. These cosmic whispers suggest a narrative of productivity and favorable circumstances throughout your professional endeavors. Engage with the hints presented by the celestial configurations, allowing their guidance to enhance your understanding and connection with the cosmic energies that shape your workday plans.

24 Saturday

When the Sun forms a harmonious trine aspect with Pluto, it empowers you to tap into your power and transform parts of your life. This aspect brings a deep self-awareness and the ability to make positive changes. You may experience a heightened sense of purpose and determination, allowing you to navigate challenges with resilience. With the Moon entering Taurus, you are encouraged to ground yourself and find stability in your emotions.

25 Sunday

Saturn ingress Aries is a time to set clear boundaries, prioritize self-discipline, and take calculated risks to pursue your ambitions. This transit invites you to embrace a sense of self-mastery and cultivate a strong understanding of personal identity and independence. As Saturn moves through Aries, you can develop inner strength and resilience while learning valuable lessons about leadership, self-reliance, and taking ownership of your actions.

MAY

26 Monday

Mercury ingress Gemini transit enhances your communication skills, making it easier to express your thoughts and ideas with clarity and precision. Mercury's sextile with Saturn brings disciplined and focused energy to your mental pursuits, allowing you to think strategically and make sound decisions. With the Moon also entering Gemini, your emotions and intuition align with your intellectual objectives, creating a harmonious blend of logic and intuition.

27 Tuesday

During the New Moon phase, you experience a potent energy of new beginnings and fresh possibilities. It is a time of setting intentions and embarking on a transformative journey. With Mercury forming a harmonious trine with Pluto, your thoughts and ideas have a profound depth and power. You possess the ability to uncover hidden truths and gain deep insights. This alignment supports introspection, research, and revealing confidential information.

28 Wednesday

Moon ingress Cancer energy encourages you to embrace vulnerability and express and process your feelings. This lunar transit invites you to honor your emotional needs and cultivate a sense of emotional well-being. Take this opportunity to create a safe and nurturing space to recharge, reflect, and tend to your emotional needs. By honoring the Moon's ingress into Cancer, you can tap into the power of your emotions and find solace in the comfort of your own heart.

29 Thursday

Within the cosmic arena of partnerships and relationships, the Sun in Gemini adds a dynamic and communicative touch to your interactions. Your approach to one-on-one connections becomes vibrant and versatile, as the Gemini influence encourages lively conversations and the exchange of ideas. Embrace the joy of intellectual camaraderie in your relationships, appreciating the diversity of perspectives that each individual brings.

JUNE

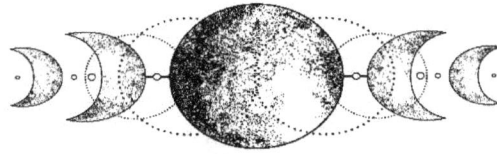

MOON MAGIC

Sun	Mon	Tue	Wed	Thu	Fri	Sat
1	2	3	4	5	6	7
8	9	10	11	12	13	14
15	16	17	18	19	20	21
22	23	24	25	26	27	28
29	30					

NEW MOON

STRAWBERRY MOON

30 Friday

As the Sun aligns with Mercury, your mind becomes sharp and focused, allowing clear communication and intellectual prowess. Your thoughts and words carry a magnetic energy that attracts attention and engages others in meaningful conversations. With the Moon moving into Leo, your confidence and self-expression amplifies. You radiate warmth and charisma, drawing people to your vibrant energy. It is a time to shine and express unique creativity and individuality.

31 Saturday

A piece of news offers a lucky break that enables you to create positive change. It brings a fortunate trend that opens your life to new people and possibilities. It draws balance and harmony into your life, and the positive aspects offer noticeable growth. It brings lively exchanges and opportunities to mingle. It emphasizes improving home and family life. You hear upbeat news on the grapevine that provides room to grow your social life.

1 Sunday

The celestial signatures inscribed in the cosmic canvas suggest a story of dynamism and cosmic nuances within your home environment. Embrace the unfolding tale written in the heavenly language, allowing the astrological landscape to guide your interpretations and actions throughout your day, inviting you to dance harmoniously with the celestial threads that shape your daily narrative across various aspects of your life.

2 Monday

As the Moon enters Virgo, you may shift your focus towards practical matters and attention to detail. This planetary ingress is when you are inclined to analyze and organize your thoughts, tasks, and surroundings. Your mind becomes attuned to efficiency and productivity, seeking ways to improve and refine your daily routines. You are naturally inclined towards precision and precision, aiming for excellence in everything you do.

3 Tuesday

Positive news disrupts your daily routine in the most uplifting way, offering you a chance to create positive changes in your lifestyle and overall well-being. This fortunate trend introduces a sense of balance and harmony into your everyday activities, leading to noticeable improvements in your health and daily routine. Embrace the positive aspects of this news as it brings lively energy to your daily exchanges and opportunities to explore new wellness practices.

4 Wednesday

Moon ingress Libra. You may desire to create beauty and surround yourself with aesthetics that inspire and uplift you. Use this energy to engage in meaningful conversations, seek compromise, and find diplomatic solutions to any conflicts or challenges that arise. By embracing the Libran qualities of fairness, diplomacy, and social grace, you can foster positive connections and create an atmosphere of harmony in your life.

5 Thursday

As Venus forms a sextile with Jupiter, you will likely experience a harmonious and expansive energy in your relationships and overall well-being. This aspect brings an optimistic outlook, allowing you to attract abundance, joy, and growth into your life. It encourages you to seek new opportunities in your personal or professional spheres and embrace the possibilities for success. Mercury's sextile with Mars fuels communicative abilities, giving you drive and assertiveness.

6 Friday

Venus in Taurus highlights the importance of stability and security in relationships and finances. You may feel a deep desire for comfort and loyalty, seeking safe and reliable relationships. This planetary transit is a time to cultivate self-worth and appreciate the simple joys in life. Honoring your desires and nurturing connections can create a solid foundation for love, abundance, and contentment. Use this time to boost desires and build a strong relationship foundation.

7 Saturday

Moon ingress Scorpio. You can delve into your emotions, seek truth, and uncover hidden desires. This transit invites you to embrace your power and dive into the mysteries of life. Your intuition and psychic abilities may be heightened during this time, allowing you to tap into unseen realms and gain deeper insights. It's a transformative period where you may experience emotional catharsis, shedding old patterns and embracing a more authentic version of yourself.

8 Sunday

When Mercury conjuncts Jupiter, it amplifies your ability to communicate, learn, and expand your horizons. Your mind is eager to absorb new information, and your curiosity knows no bounds. This alignment encourages you to seek knowledge, broaden your perspectives, and engage in meaningful conversations. Mercury's ingress into Cancer makes your communication style more intuitive, compassionate, and sensitive.

9 Monday

Venus square Pluto intensifies your relationships and emotions, bringing transformative energy to matters of the heart. It may trigger power struggles or intense emotions but also presents an opportunity for healing and growth. With Jupiter's ingress into Cancer, you enter a phase of growth and expansion. This transit encourages you to focus on your home, family, and emotional well-being. It's a time to deepen your connections and find comfort in nurturing aspects.

10 Tuesday

Celestial energies usher in a period of creative breakthroughs, offering you the chance to make a significant impact through your artistic endeavors. This cosmic influence creates a fortunate trend that opens your life to new creative expressions and possibilities. Embrace the harmonious balance that these energies bring to your creative pursuits, and notice how the positive aspects of this celestial alignment contribute to the growth and expansion of your artistic talents.

11 Wednesday

Full Moon. Mercury sextile Venus. It's a good time for creative expression and engaging in activities that bring joy and beauty. Embrace the energy of the Full Moon and the supportive alignment of Mercury and Venus as they encourage you to express yourself authentically and cultivate harmonious connections with those around you. It's a time to embrace love, creativity, and the abundant possibilities that lie before you.

12 Thursday

Moon ingress Capricorn. The Moon in Capricorn invites you to embrace your inner strength and resilience, reminding you of your ability to overcome challenges and reach new heights. It's a time to align your emotions with your aspirations and make strategic decisions that support your growth and stability. Use this energy to cultivate a solid foundation for your dreams and take steps towards your desired achievements.

13 Friday

As the cosmic tapestry weaves on Friday the 13th, the celestial threads intertwine to create an atmosphere charged with unique energies. The cosmic currents suggest a day of introspection and heightened intuition, encouraging you to trust your instincts and delve into the deeper layers of your consciousness. Embrace the cosmic dance of this Friday, the 13th, recognizing the potential for heavenly revelations and a deeper understanding of your celestial path.

14 Saturday

Your emotions may become more detached and objective, allowing you to observe and analyze situations with a fresh perspective. It is an excellent time to engage in group activities and connect with like-minded individuals. Embrace your individuality and embrace the freedom to express your unique ideas and beliefs. Allow the Moon in Aquarius to inspire you to think outside the box and positively impact your community and the world.

15 Sunday

When Mars squares Uranus and Jupiter squares Saturn, you may experience conflict between your desire for freedom and your need for stability. This combination of planetary aspects can create a sense of restlessness and a strong urge for change and independence. This alignment can be a time of breakthroughs as you navigate between your desire for expansion and the limitations imposed by external circumstances.

16 Monday

Moon ingress Pisces. Take time to nourish your soul and engage in activities that bring you joy and peace. Please pay attention to your intuition, as it can guide you toward the right path and help you navigate any challenges. Allow yourself to be compassionate towards yourself and others, as this is a time of increased empathy and understanding. Embrace Pisces's gentle and reflective energy and let it guide you on a journey of self-discovery and spiritual growth.

17 Tuesday

When Mars ingresses Virgo, you benefit from increasing practical and detail-oriented energy. Virgo is an earth sign known for its precision and efficiency, and with Mars in this sign, you are motivated to take action systematically and organized. This period encourages you to pay attention to the small details and work diligently towards your goals. You may desire to improve your daily routines, health, and productivity.

18 Wednesday

When the Moon ingress Aries, you feel a surge of energy and assertiveness. Aries is a fire sign known for its boldness, enthusiasm, and drive. During this time, you may feel increased confidence and desire to take initiative in various areas of your life. Your emotions are more spontaneous and passionate, and you're ready to tackle challenges head-on. This transition is a time for action and embracing new beginnings.

19 Thursday

Jupiter square Neptune. By staying grounded and maintaining a realistic perspective, you can navigate with greater wisdom and make conscious choices that align with your values. Embrace a practical and pragmatic approach while still keeping your dreams alive, finding ways to bridge the gap between your ideals and the actualities of life. Remember to trust in your inner wisdom and intuition as you navigate the complexities of this planetary aspect.

20 Friday

An enchanting chapter brings a shift forward that directs your energy towards a path that offers room to grow your life. It plants the seeds for an exciting journey to unfold. Mingling with your circle of friends brings heightened activity and invitations. New potential sweeps in, moving you forward towards a stable chapter of growing your social life. It brings a slow and steady transformation that offers personal growth and connection.

21 Saturday

When the Moon ingresses into Taurus and the Sun ingresses into Cancer, it marks the June Solstice, a significant turning point in the year. You may feel a deep connection to the Earth and a desire for stability and security. The nurturing energy of Cancer combined with Taurus's grounded nature brings comfort and familiarity. You may find yourself seeking solace in life's simple pleasures, enjoying the beauty of nature, and nurturing your relationships and home life.

22 Sunday

Mars sextile Jupiter. Sun square Saturn. It's a time to assess your commitments, responsibilities, and long-term plans, ensuring they align with your authentic desires and values. While you may encounter delays or restrictions, remember that they can serve as valuable lessons and stepping stones toward your ultimate success. Use the Mars-Jupiter sextile to tap into your inner drive and determination, and approach the Sun-Saturn square with a resilient attitude.

23 Monday

Moon ingress Gemini. Sun square Neptune. Embrace the versatility and adaptability of Gemini, allowing yourself to engage in new ideas and perspectives while remaining grounded in reality. By consciously navigating the Sun-Neptune square, you can find the balance between your creative aspirations and the practical steps needed to manifest them. Stay present, maintain clear boundaries, and cultivate a discerning mindset to maximize this lunar phase.

24 Tuesday

When the Sun aligns with Jupiter in conjunction, you infuse with optimism, expansion, and abundance. This celestial connection amplifies your confidence and encourages you to embrace growth and personal development opportunities. You may feel a renewed sense of purpose and an eagerness to explore new horizons. The expansive energy of Jupiter helps you tap into your potential and encourages you to aim high, dream big, and take bold steps toward your goals.

25 Wednesday

Moon ingress Cancer. New Moon. Use this lunar cycle to reflect on your desires, set meaningful goals, and take steps toward manifesting your dreams. The New Moon in Cancer holds the potential for emotional healing, deep self-reflection, and the opportunity to establish a solid foundation for your personal and domestic life. Embrace the gentle energy of this New Moon as you embark on a journey of self-discovery and emotional growth.

26 Thursday

With Mercury forming a harmonious sextile with Uranus and the Sun in a supportive sextile with Mars, there is an electric and dynamic energy in the air. You are encouraged to embrace your unique ideas and express yourself with confidence. The Mercury-Uranus sextile sparks innovative thinking and opens doors to new possibilities. Your sharp mind inspires you to think outside the box and take risks.

27 Friday

With the Moon shifting into Leo, you can embrace your inner radiance and express your unique sense of self. The fiery energy of Leo ignites your passions and inspires you to shine brightly in the world. Tap into your creativity, confidence, and leadership qualities and allow your authentic self to take center stage and share your gifts and talents with others. Embrace the playful and joyful spirit of Leo as you embark on adventures and explore avenues of self-expression.

28 Saturday

With Mercury forming a harmonious trine aspect to Saturn and Neptune, you open a powerful blend of practicality and imagination. This combination allows you to clearly and deeply communicate your ideas and visions. Your thoughts and words are grounded in practicality, enabling you to bring structure and organization to your plans and goals. At the same time, your mind is attuned to the realms of intuition and creativity, allowing you to tap into your imagination.

29 Sunday

Mercury opposed Pluto alignment can bring power struggles and a strong desire for control and dominance. You may engage in deep and probing conversations, seeking the truth and uncovering hidden information. Be mindful of your communication style during this time, as there is a tendency for confrontations and arguments. Virgo's precision and analytical nature can help you stay grounded and focused amidst the intensity.

JULY

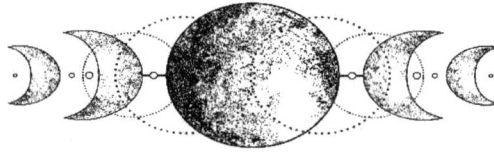

MOON MAGIC

Sun	Mon	Tue	Wed	Thu	Fri	Sat
		1	2	3	4	5
6	7	8	9	10	11	12
13	14	15	16	17	18	19
20	21	22	23	24	25	26
27	28	29	30	31		

SAGITTARIUS

NEW MOON

_____

_____

_____

_____

_____

_____

_____

_____

_____

_____

_____

_____

_____

_____

_____

_____

_____

_____

_____

_____

_____

BUCK MOON

30 Monday

A gateway ahead opens new opportunities. It brings fresh energy, which rejuvenates your surroundings and offers a lighter path forward in your life. It helps you find your feet on firm ground as you develop new projects and endeavors that inspire your creativity. Improving life draws a significant influence that encourages growth and learning. It brings a new possibility that draws excitement as you get busy expanding the borders of your world.

1 Tuesday

When the Moon enters Libra, you may feel like creating harmony and balance in your relationships and surroundings. You have a heightened awareness of the needs and perspectives of others, which can lead to a greater emphasis on cooperation and compromise. Your focus shifts to seeking peace, fairness, and diplomacy in your interactions. It is a favorable time for socializing, networking, and engaging in activities that promote collaboration and teamwork.

2 Wednesday

Improvement ahead cracks the code to building stable foundations in your life. It brings a winning chapter that draws many blessings into your world. An influence emerging helps you develop some dreams you've had on the back burner. Getting involved in progressing your vision forward illustrates a sunny aspect that brings inspiration into your life. News arrives that brings a boost and leaves you feeling excited about the potential around your life.

3 Thursday

An advantageous development in your professional realm unfolds, presenting a golden opportunity for positive change. This news initiates a stroke of luck that opens doors to new connections and possibilities in your work life. The cosmic currents bring a sense of balance and harmony to your career path, and the positive aspects of this development pave the way for noticeable growth and advancement in your professional journey.

4 Friday

When the Moon enters Scorpio, you can dive deep into the realms of your emotions and explore the hidden depths of your psyche. This astrological transit brings intensity and passion to your experiences as you seek to uncover the truth and delve into matters of the heart. The Scorpio Moon encourages you to embrace transformation and release what no longer serves you, allowing personal growth and healing.

5 Saturday

In the depths of transformation and shared resources, the Sun in Cancer brings nurturing and protective energy to the mysteries of the eighth house. Your approach to intimate connections and joint ventures becomes emotionally charged and deeply connected to the bonds of family. Embrace the joy of exploring the profound depths of shared experiences and finding satisfaction in the nurturing aspects of shared resources.

6 Sunday

When Venus forms a sextile with Saturn, you may experience a harmonious blend of love and responsibility. This aspect brings stability and practicality to your relationships, allowing you to build solid foundations based on trust and commitment. It's a time to take a realistic approach to matters of the heart and make thoughtful decisions that promote long-term happiness. Venus sextiles Neptune; compassion and empathy infuse your interactions with others.

7 Monday

Uranus ingress Gemini transit brings a fresh and innovative energy that encourages you to embrace new ideas, perspectives, and ways of relating to others. Your mind becomes more open to unconventional and revolutionary concepts, and you may find yourself drawn to explore various forms of self-expression and intellectual pursuits. Meanwhile, the Venus trine Pluto aspect deepens your connections and brings transformative experiences to relationships and values.

8 Tuesday

Your approach to joint ventures and shared financial matters is marked by emotional intelligence and a deep understanding of the intricacies involved. The Sun in Cancer encourages you to bring nurturing and protective energy to your financial dealings, creating an environment where trust and emotional security thrive. Your career experiences transformative growth when you embrace shared resources with compassionate and intuitive Cancer.

9 Wednesday

Moon ingress Capricorn. You may find yourself drawn to activities that promote stability and achievement, and you can make significant strides in your professional and personal endeavors. Use this time to prioritize your responsibilities, establish solid foundations, and work diligently towards your aspirations. By embracing the practical energy of Capricorn, you can achieve tangible results and lay the groundwork for future success.

10 Thursday

During the Full Moon, you may experience heightened emotions and illumination. This lunar phase signifies a culmination and completion of a cycle, shedding light on areas of your life that require attention and reflection. It's a time to embrace your inner wisdom and intuition as the Full Moon amplifies your emotions and brings them to the surface. You may feel a stronger connection to your authentic self and a deeper understanding of your needs and desires.

11 Friday

When the Moon enters Aquarius, you may express individuality and uniqueness. It's a time to embrace your eccentricities and the freedom to be yourself. You may desire to connect with like-minded individuals and engage in intellectual pursuits. This energy encourages you to think outside the box, challenge the status quo, and explore innovative ideas. It's a time to tap into your humanitarian side and contribute to causes that align with your values.

12 Saturday

Positive developments unfold in your home and family life, bringing a fortunate trend that opens new avenues for improvement and growth. The cosmic energies draw a sense of balance and harmony into your domestic sphere, emphasizing positive aspects that contribute to the overall well-being of your home life. Expect upbeat news on the grapevine that provides room to enhance your familial bonds and create a more harmonious and joyful living environment.

13 Sunday

When Saturn turns retrograde, it invites you to reflect on your responsibilities, limitations, and long-term goals. This transit is a period for introspection and inner work, where you can reassess your commitments and the structures you have in place. It's a time to evaluate whether they align with your aspirations and values. With the Moon entering Pisces, your emotions may become more intuitive and empathetic.

14 Monday

In a piece of uplifting news, a fortunate turn of events offers a lucky break in your professional journey, allowing you to instigate positive change. This promising trend opens avenues to connect with new colleagues and explore fresh possibilities in your work life. The cosmic currents usher in balance and harmony, and the positive aspects promise significant growth and advancement in your career. Trusting your instincts guides you towards growing your knowledge.

15 Tuesday

Visualizing your goals today heightens the essence of manifestation around your life. The more you listen to your intuition, the more you trust yourself to guide you towards the right journey for your situation. You make a decision that feels like the right choice for your circumstances. This path encourages you to expand your skillset and extend your reach into a new area of learning and wisdom. You have the opportunity to access higher education and advance to a growth area.

16 Wednesday

Moon ingress Aries. Trust your instincts and follow your passion as you navigate this dynamic and energetic period. Use the assertive energy of Aries to initiate new beginnings, take risks, and embrace a proactive approach to life. This proactive transit is your time to step forward, be bold, and make things happen. Remember to channel this energy wisely, staying mindful of your actions and considering their impact on yourself and others.

17 Thursday

You discover an open road of exciting options that tempt you forward. It brings a burst of sunshine into your world. It offers new possibilities that help you power ahead using skills and abilities. Newfound motivation fuels inspiration and enables you to launch into a new chapter of significant gains for your life. It leads to a richly creative environment that sets up a stable foundation from which to grow your life outwardly.

18 Friday

When Mercury turns retrograde, you may experience a shift in communication and a need for introspection. It's a time to review and reflect on your thoughts, ideas, and plans. As the Moon moves into Taurus, you seek stability and a grounded approach. It can be a supportive time for connecting with your senses and finding comfort in the present moment. With Mercury sextile Venus, there is an opportunity to enhance your relationships and creative expression.

19 Saturday

News arrives that expands your circle of friends. It offers a group environment and a chance to work with your creative abilities. A river of unique possibilities emerges in your broader social network, which becomes the gateway from which you grow your life. A positive influence reverberates around your life as it brings new options to your door. Your social schedule fills up with opportunities to mingle.

20 Sunday

Moon ingress Gemini is a favorable period for learning, gathering information, and expanding your knowledge in various areas of interest. Your intellectual curiosity awakens, and you may seek new experiences and perspectives. Embrace the versatility of Gemini energy and allow yourself to adapt and flow with the changing tides of your thoughts and emotions. This transit is a time to explore, communicate, and embrace the joy of intellectual exchange.

21 Monday

Upbeat news disrupts your daily routine in the most uplifting way, providing a lucky break to create positive changes in your lifestyle and overall well-being. This fortunate trend introduces balance and harmony into your everyday activities, leading to noticeable improvements in your health and daily routine. Embrace the positive aspects of this news, as it brings lively exchanges, promoting a healthier and more harmonious lifestyle.

22 Tuesday

As the Moon moves into Cancer, you may feel a shift towards emotional sensitivity and nurturing energies. It is a time to focus on self-care, create a comforting environment, and connect deeply with your emotions. Allow yourself to be guided by your intuition and inner wisdom as you navigate your personal and domestic life. With the Sun entering Leo, there is a spotlight on self-expression, confidence, and creative pursuits.

23 Wednesday

As the Sun forms a sextile with Uranus, you may experience a surge of innovative energy and a desire for change. This cosmic aspect encourages you to embrace individuality, break free from routine, and explore new possibilities. You are likely to feel a sense of excitement and openness to unique experiences and perspectives. However, the Venus square Mars aspect may bring some tension and conflict in your relationships or personal desires.

24 Thursday

With the Sun trine Saturn, you reveal steady and disciplined energy that allows you to manifest your goals and ambitions with practicality and determination. This aspect empowers you to take responsibility for your actions and make steady progress toward your long-term aspirations. As the Moon ingresses Leo, it infuses you with confidence, self-expression, and creativity. With the New Moon, a fresh cycle begins, allowing you to set new intentions.

25 Friday

The sun-opposed Pluto aspect brings forth a power struggle between your ego and deeper, subconscious forces. It's a time of potential conflict and confrontation within yourself and your interactions with others. The Sun represents your core identity, and Pluto symbolizes the forces of transformation and regeneration. Under this influence, you may encounter power struggles, control issues, or intense emotions that challenge your sense of self.

26 Saturday

Moon ingress Virgo energy encourages you to focus on practical matters, efficiency, and productivity. It's when you can bring a sense of order and structure to your daily routines and tasks. You may find yourself drawn to caring for your physical well-being, organizing your workspace, or engaging in activities promoting health and cleanliness. This transit also highlights the importance of self-care and self-improvement.

27 Sunday

Positive developments grace your home and family life, bringing a fortunate trend that opens doors to improvements and growth. The cosmic energies introduce balance and harmony into your domestic sphere, emphasizing positive aspects that contribute to the overall well-being of your home life. Expect upbeat news on the grapevine that provides room to enhance familial bonds, creating a more harmonious and joyful living environment.

28 Monday

Moving towards growing your talents does see you create progress in developing your vision. You are ready to turn the dial towards growth. You can make headway on your goals by combining proactive measures and planning your strategy. You discover you can make tracks and achieve traction on a long-awaited dream. It takes you on a path of adventure and lets you transition to an environment that holds great promise.

29 Tuesday

As the Moon enters Libra, you feel a shift toward seeking balance and harmony in your relationships and surroundings. This period encourages you to consider the needs and perspectives of others, fostering a desire for cooperation and fairness in your interactions. You may find yourself drawn to socializing, connecting with others, and appreciating art, beauty, and the finer things in life. During this transit, you may enjoy engaging in artistic activities that nourish your soul.

30 Wednesday

Celestial inspirations ignite innovative breakthroughs, introducing a fortunate trend that expands your creative horizons. This positive news draws balance and harmony into your creative pursuits, propelling growth and recognition for your artistic talents. Expect lively exchanges and opportunities to collaborate with fellow creatives, creating an atmosphere of inspiration and fostering the evolution of your creative expression.

31 Thursday

The Sun's conjunction with Mercury enhances your communication skills and mental clarity, allowing you to express your thoughts and ideas readily. This alignment fosters intellectual curiosity and the desire to engage in stimulating conversations. Use this time to embrace emotional vulnerability and open communication as you explore the depths of your emotions and connections with others.

AUGUST

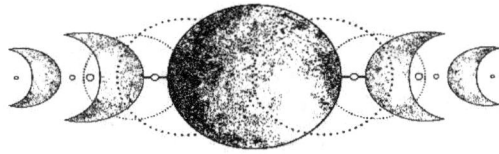

MOON MAGIC

Sun	Mon	Tue	Wed	Thu	Fri	Sat
					1	2
3	4	5	6	7	8	9
10	11	12	13	14	15	16
17	18	19	20	21	22	23
24	25	26	27	28	29	30
31						

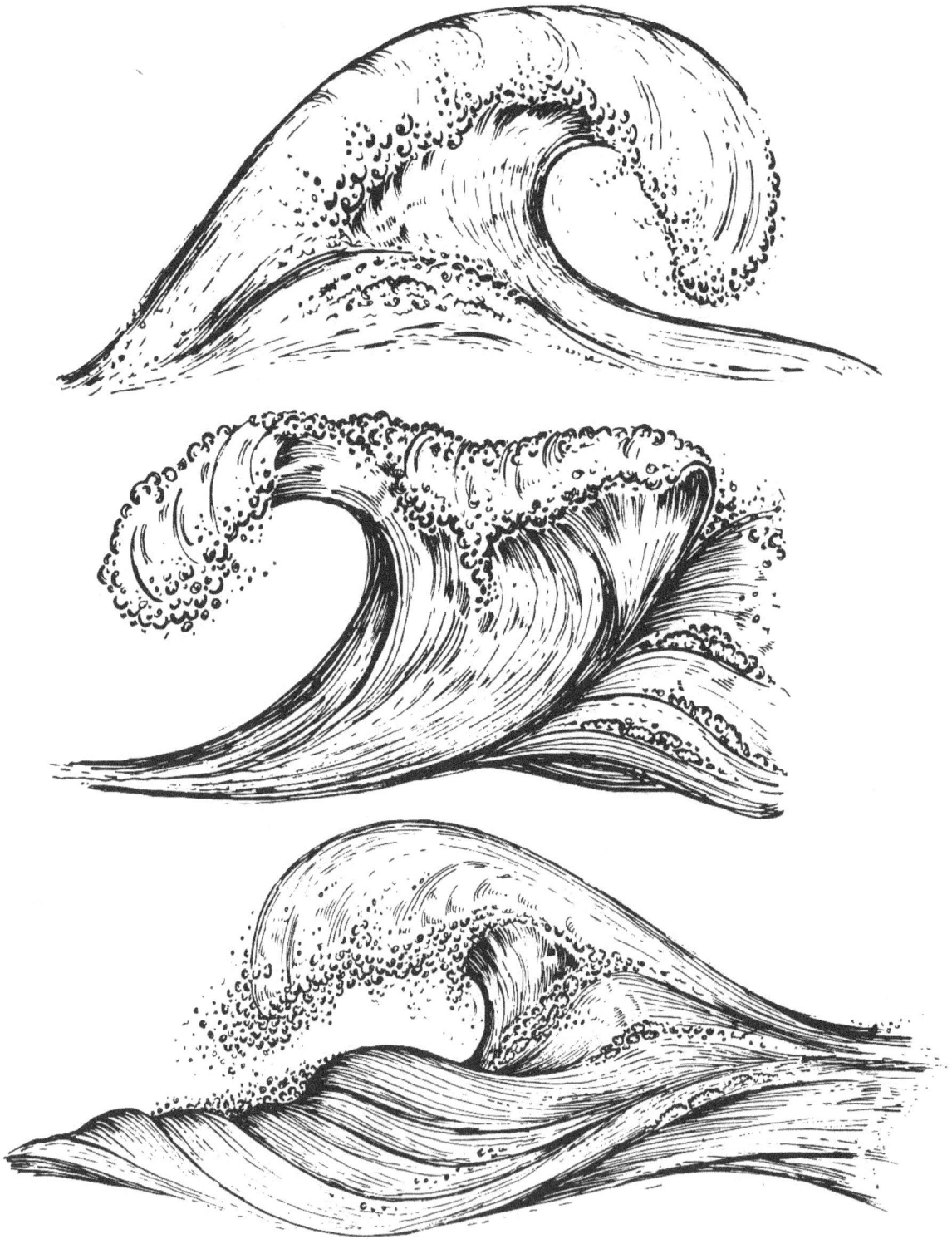

NEW MOON

_____

_____

_____

_____

_____

_____

_____

_____

_____

_____

_____

_____

_____

_____

_____

_____

_____

_____

STURGEON MOON

_____

_____

_____

_____

_____

_____

_____

_____

_____

_____

_____

_____

_____

_____

_____

_____

_____

_____

AUGUST

1 Friday

When Venus forms a square aspect with Saturn and Neptune, you might experience challenges in your relationships and emotional life. This aspect can create a sense of tension and restriction, making it difficult to express your feelings and desires fully. You may need to confront specific issues or limitations within your partnerships or connections with others. Being realistic and honest about your expectations and boundaries is essential.

2 Saturday

With the Sun illuminating your expansive ninth house, your Leo energy is fueled by a thirst for adventure. You approach life with enthusiasm, seeking experiences that allow you to express your creativity and individuality on a grand scale. Your natural charisma draws you to explore different cultures and philosophies, and you may find joy in sharing your wisdom with others. Be cautious not to let a tendency for self-righteousness hinder your openness to diverse perspectives.

3 Sunday

When the Moon moves into Sagittarius, you may feel adventurous and desire to explore new horizons. This transit can boost optimism and enthusiasm, encouraging you to embrace new challenges and growth opportunities. Your curiosity might be piqued, and you may find yourself drawn to learning, traveling, or expanding your knowledge in various ways. This transit is a time to broaden your horizons and embrace the spirit of adventure.

4 Monday

Exploring leads and researching options helps you come up with a winning trajectory. It provides you with an approach that lets you chase your vision for future growth. You soon build stable foundations that heighten the security in your life. Climbing the rungs ahead sees you reaching for success. It does allow things to move forward quickly as you draw a stable foundation from which to grow your vision.

5 Tuesday

Moon ingress Capricorn is a time to set realistic and achievable targets and approach tasks with a vital purpose. Embrace the energy of Capricorn to organize your priorities, make wise decisions, and build a solid foundation for your future endeavors. Use this lunar phase to tap into your inner strength and perseverance, and you'll find yourself making steady progress toward your aspirations. This transit encourages you to focus on goals and take practical steps to achieve them.

6 Wednesday

Mars ingress Libra transit encourages you to approach conflicts diplomatically and fairly, seeking compromises and win-win solutions. You might feel drawn to collaboration and teamwork, valuing cooperation and considering the needs of others as you pursue your objectives. It is a time to build connections and find common ground with those around you. You might also be more inclined to seek beauty and aesthetics in your surroundings, appreciating art and design.

7 Thursday

Curious news arrives that provides a side option. It brings inspiration flowing into your world. Golden threads of potential weave magic around your life. It takes you towards a transition where you can clear the decks and embrace a fresh chapter of potential. Overall, rejuvenation is a theme that resonates with abundance in your life. It brings a turning point that lifts your spirit and adds the right flavor to the spice of life.

8 Friday

With the Moon entering Aquarius and Mars forming a trine with Uranus, you might experience a surge of energy and a desire for greater freedom and independence. During this time, you may feel more inclined to break free from routine and embrace new and unconventional ideas. This astrological combination can ignite your innovative spirit, pushing you to explore unique approaches to challenges and tasks.

9 Saturday

With Mars forming oppositions with Saturn and Neptune and a Full Moon illuminating the skies, you may feel a mix of challenges and heightened emotions. Mars opposed Saturn can bring about a sense of frustration or delays in pursuing your goals, requiring you to exercise patience and discipline in overcoming obstacles. The Full Moon amplifies emotions and may bring hidden feelings to the surface, prompting you to examine your needs and desires more closely.

10 Sunday

With the Moon moving into dreamy Pisces and Mars forming a harmonious trine with transformative Pluto, you may experience a day filled with deep emotions and powerful motivation. This transit is a time to tap into your intuition and explore your subconscious desires and feelings. You might draw creative and spiritual pursuits, seeking meaning and connection in your experiences. The Mars-Pluto trine empowers you with inner strength and determination.

11 Monday

As Mercury turns direct, you may feel a sense of relief and clarity after a period of potential communication challenges and miscommunications. This shift in Mercury's direction signals a time for smoother interactions, improved decision-making, and a greater sense of mental clarity. It's an opportune moment to tie up loose ends, finalize plans, and move forward with any projects or ideas delayed during its retrograde phase.

12 Tuesday

With Saturn sextile Uranus, you may find a harmonious balance between stability and change. This cosmic aspect encourages you to embrace innovation and progress while maintaining a solid foundation. You can create positive transformations in various areas of your life, especially regarding long-term goals and plans. At the same time, the conjunction of Venus and Jupiter brings a sense of abundance, joy, and positivity to your relationships and experiences.

13 Wednesday

A new possibility crops up and brings an enterprising chapter that offers stable foundations. Your life lights up with new potential, and taking matters into your own hands draws a fruitful result. A decisive time enables you to reach for your dreams proactively. It helps you go after a high-level assignment that deepens your talents and refines your skills. It reveals an area that holds promise for your working life.

14 Thursday

With the Moon in Taurus, you may experience a sense of groundedness and stability. This transit focuses on the material and practical aspects, encouraging you to find comfort in the simple pleasures and indulge in sensory delights. You may seek to establish a harmonious environment around you. Your emotions will likely be steady and reliable during this period, and you may find solace in spending time in nature or engaging in creative and pleasurable activities.

15 Friday

Mercury sextile Mars enhances your ability to articulate your thoughts and ideas confidently and assertively. Your mind is sharp and quick, allowing you to think on your feet and easily make decisions. This transit is an excellent time for initiating conversations, negotiations, or expressing your opinions, as your words carry a potent impact. You may also feel more motivated to take action on your ideas and plans, as Mars fuels your drive and determination.

16 Saturday

Moon ingress Gemini influence encourages you to engage in lively conversations and seek new experiences and information. Your mind is agile, and you are open to exploring various perspectives and ideas. It's an excellent time to connect, share your thoughts, and listen to what they say. Your communication skills heighten, making expressing yourself with charm and wit easier. Embrace the lightheartedness of Gemini and enjoy the mental stimulation it brings.

17 Sunday

A stroke of luck enhances your social life as uplifting news spreads, creating a fortunate trend that opens doors to new people and social possibilities. The cosmic energies draw balance and harmony into your social interactions, fostering positive growth in your relationships. Embrace the lively exchanges and opportunities to mingle that come with this news, emphasizing the improvement of your connections and cultivating a more vibrant and fulfilling social circle.

18 Monday

As Mercury forms a harmonious sextile with Mars, you may find your communication style becomes more assertive and direct. This alignment encourages you to express your thoughts and ideas confidently and clearly, making it easier for others to understand your intentions. Additionally, with the Moon moving into Cancer, you might experience heightened emotional sensitivity and nurturing energy.

19 Tuesday

Focusing on improving your career path draws improvement. You enter a phase that sees growth and stability take shape. It advances your job prospects and sees you join a dynamic chapter ahead. Adjusting and refining your goals draws a productive chapter. You streamline your working life into an efficient powerhouse that lets you reach your goals with purpose. It helps create progress; information ahead brings insight into the blocks currently holding you back.

20 Wednesday

As the Moon enters the passionate sign of Leo, you may infuse with a sense of creativity and self-expression. Your emotions take on a dramatic flair, and you desire to be noticed and appreciated. This Leo influence encourages you to embrace your inner performer and shine brightly in any social setting. You'll be inclined to seek out activities that bring joy and excitement, and your generous and enthusiastic nature will likely draw people toward you.

21 Thursday

A fresh cycle beckons; the time is right to move forward and head towards expansion in your life. You are ready to engage with the broader world of potential. Serendipity lights the way towards a social aspect that brings new friends and companions into your world. It shines a light on friendship and happiness. Opportunities to engage with your circle of friends get lively discussions and a practical sense of well-being.

22 Friday

Sun ingress Virgo. This transit is an excellent time to pay attention to your health and well-being, as Virgo's energy supports wellness and self-care. Embrace this transit's earthy and grounded nature, as it can help you lay the groundwork for future success and personal growth. Utilize this period to refine your skills, address any lingering issues, and implement positive changes that will serve you well in the days ahead.

23 Saturday

With the Moon's ingress into Virgo, combined with the energy of the New Moon, you may experience a period of introspection and practicality. It is a time for setting new intentions and initiating fresh starts. Your focus turns towards analyzing and organizing various aspects of your daily routines and habits, seeking ways to improve efficiency and productivity. Virgo's influence encourages you to pay attention to the finer details and strive for perfection in your endeavors.

24 Sunday

With the Sun forming a square aspect to Uranus, you might experience a surge of unpredictability and restlessness. This planetary alignment challenges you to break from routines and embrace a more unconventional approach to situations. You may find yourself seeking independence and craving excitement, which could lead to sudden changes or unexpected events. While this period might bring excitement and innovation, it's essential to be mindful of impulsive decisions.

25 Monday

Moon ingress Libra. Venus ingress Leo. You'll be drawn towards creating a peaceful and pleasant atmosphere, seeking common ground with others, and resolving conflicts. The Libra influence encourages you to consider the needs and perspectives of those around you, fostering a cooperative and fair approach in your interactions. At the same time, Venus in Leo ignites your desire for warmth, admiration, and affection in your romantic connections.

26 Tuesday

The sextile to Uranus adds a touch of excitement and spontaneity, encouraging you to explore new avenues of romance and social connections. Additionally, the trine to Neptune enhances your sensitivity and imagination, allowing you to express your feelings with greater empathy. This celestial configuration supports grounded love and open-mindedness, making it a promising time to find a balance between the familiar and the thrilling aspects of your emotional experiences.

27 Wednesday

As Venus opposes Pluto, you might encounter intense emotions and power struggles in your relationships and interactions. This astrological aspect can bring hidden issues and underlying tensions to the surface, potentially leading to feelings of jealousy, possessiveness, or control. Be cautious of engaging in manipulative behaviors or getting entangled in situations that could become toxic. Maintaining open communication and honesty to navigate through this period is crucial.

28 Thursday

Moon ingress Scorpio. This lunar transit encourages you to delve into your feelings and thoughts with a more profound and investigative approach. You might find yourself drawn to explore hidden or taboo subjects, seeking a better understanding of the deeper layers of your psyche. Scorpio's influence can bring out a sense of heightened intuition and increased sensitivity, making it a good time for introspection and self-reflection.

29 Friday

Uranus sextile Neptune. This harmonious connection between Uranus and Neptune offers an excellent opportunity to bridge the gap between practicality and spirituality, bringing a sense of unity and interconnectedness to your experiences. Embrace this period of cosmic synergy to explore your unique vision and find innovative ways to express your artistic and spiritual pursuits, enriching your life with a more profound sense of purpose and meaning.

30 Saturday

Moon ingress Sagittarius. You might feel a strong urge to break free from routines and constraints and, instead, embrace spontaneity and take on challenges enthusiastically. During this period, you may find yourself drawn to activities that involve travel, learning, or spiritual exploration. Embrace the Sagittarian energy to fuel your curiosity, embrace change, and find more profound meaning and purpose in your experiences.

31 Sunday

A more social environment promotes expansion in your life. It places you in contact with unique friends and helps you move forward towards chasing your dreams. Shaking off the heavy vibrations releases stress and creates space for exciting possibilities in your life. It is an ideal time to direct your energy toward growing your social life. Group activities ahead bring news and excitement to the forefront as they open a door forward in your life.

SEPTEMBER

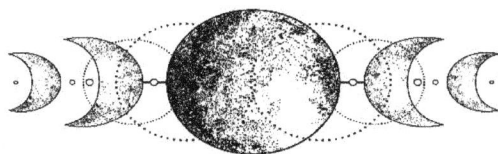

MOON MAGIC

Sun	Mon	Tue	Wed	Thu	Fri	Sat
	1	2	3	4	5	6
7	8	9	10	11	12	13
14	15	16	17	18	19	20
21	22	23	24	25	26	27
28	29	30				

NEW MOON

Corn/Harvest Moon

September

1 Monday

With Saturn's ingress into Pisces, you may experience a shift in your approach to discipline, responsibility, and spiritual growth. Pisces' influence brings more reflective and compassionate energy, prompting you to delve into your inner world and explore matters of faith and higher consciousness. During this period, you might find that your practical side merges with a more profound sensitivity, allowing you to approach challenges with empathy and understanding.

2 Tuesday

The Moon in Capricorn brings a sense of responsibility and a focus on long-term goals, encouraging you to be disciplined and persistent in pursuing your ambitions. Your emotions may become more reserved, and you might find it easier to detach from intense feelings, allowing for a more rational perspective. With Mercury in Virgo, your communication style becomes more precise and analytical, making it excellent for organizing and conveying your thoughts.

3 Wednesday

Mercury square Uranus. While this energy can be refreshing, staying grounded and avoiding jumping to conclusions without thorough consideration is essential. Embrace the opportunity to explore new perspectives and embrace your uniqueness, but also be mindful of the potential for misunderstandings or communication breakdowns. During this time, strive to find a healthy balance between your need for novelty and the practicality of effective communication.

4 Thursday

Moon ingress Aquarius. Your emotions may be more objective and detached, allowing you to approach situations with a broader perspective. It's a favorable time to engage in intellectual pursuits and exchange ideas with like-minded individuals. Embrace the innovative and open-minded energy of the Aquarius Moon, and use it as an opportunity to connect with others meaningfully, positively impacting your relationships and the wider community.

5 Friday

With Mars forming a square aspect to Jupiter, you may experience a surge of energy and enthusiasm. Still, it's essential to be mindful of potential excesses and impulsivity during this time. The dynamic combination of Mars and Jupiter can lead to a strong desire for growth and expansion, motivating you to take on new challenges and pursue your goals with great zeal. However, be cautious not to overextend yourself or take on more than you can handle.

6 Saturday

With the Moon's ingress into Pisces, your emotions may become more intuitive and compassionate. This lunar transit encourages you to tap into your creative and empathetic side, fostering a deeper connection with your feelings and those of others. It's a favorable time for introspective activities, artistic pursuits, and acts of kindness. Embrace the combined energies of Uranus turning retrograde and the Moon in Pisces to embark on inner transformation and emotional awareness.

7 Sunday

The Full Moon can amplify your intuition and bring clarity to your emotions, helping you gain deeper insights into your inner world. It's a decisive moment to set intentions for personal growth and transformation, harnessing the energy of the Full Moon to manifest your desires and bring them to fruition. Embrace this potent lunar phase as an opportunity for self-reflection, letting go, and embracing positive change in your life.

8 Monday

Moon ingress Aries lunar transit can ignite a sense of courage and a desire to take on new challenges enthusiastically. You might find yourself drawn to assert independence and pursue your passions with renewed purpose. Aries' influence encourages you to express your desires and initiate action boldly. It's a favorable time to start new projects. Channel the dynamic energy of the Aries Moon into constructive activities and allow it to fuel your motivation and drive for growth.

9 Tuesday

The Sun in Virgo graces your tenth house, emphasizing your diligent and service-oriented approach to your career and public image. You are driven to achieve success through precision and dedication, often finding fulfillment in roles that allow you to apply your analytical skills. Your attention to detail and strong work ethic contribute to your reputation as a reliable and efficient professional. Acknowledge your accomplishments with the same approach.

10 Wednesday

As the Moon enters Taurus, you may experience a shift towards a more grounded and stable emotional state. Taurus' influence brings a sense of comfort and appreciation for the simple pleasures of life. During this lunar transit, you might seek security and stability in your surroundings and relationships. You may notice a stronger connection to nature and a desire to indulge in sensory experiences, such as savoring delicious food or enjoying soothing sounds and scents.

11 Thursday

The wheels are in motion; it involves investigating options and embarking on an entire growth cycle. Life aligns favorably, creating a shift forward. It makes way for a brighter future where you are in the driver's seat and can create positive change. An exciting possibility leaves you feeling inspired and keen to step forward and progress the potential possible. It opens a path of learning and growth that advances your journey onward.

12 Friday

With the Sun forming a sextile aspect to Jupiter, you may experience positive energy and optimism, inspiring you to expand your horizons and seek new growth opportunities. This astrological alignment encourages you to embrace a more expansive and open-minded approach. As the Moon moves into Gemini, you might find your emotions becoming more curious and adaptable, prompting you to engage in lively conversations and explore diverse interests.

13 Saturday

The Sun is conjunct Mercury; you may experience rising mental clarity and communication abilities. During this alignment, your thoughts and self-expression are in sync, making it easier to articulate your ideas and convey your thoughts confidently. This astrological aspect enhances your intellectual prowess and can lead to greater self-awareness. It's a time to trust your intuition and tap into your inner wisdom, as your mind is sharp and receptive to new information.

14 Sunday

Upbeat news disrupts your daily habits in a positive light, providing a fortunate break to instigate changes in your lifestyle and overall well-being. This trend introduces balance and harmony into your daily activities, leading to noticeable improvements in your health and routines. Embrace the positive aspects as you navigate lively exchanges and opportunities to explore new wellness practices, promoting a healthier and more harmonious lifestyle.

15 Monday

As the Moon moves into Cancer, you may notice a shift in your emotional landscape, becoming more attuned to your feelings and those of others. Cancer's influence brings a nurturing and sensitive energy, encouraging you to seek comfort and security in your surroundings. During this lunar transit, you might feel more of a need for emotional connection and a desire to create a harmonious home environment.

16 Tuesday

With Venus forming a sextile aspect to Mars, you may experience a harmonious blend of passion and affection in your relationships and interactions. This astrological alignment brings balance and ease in expressing your desires and emotions. Your romantic and social energies are in sync, allowing you to attract positive and loving experiences. During this period, you might feel more confident and assertive in pursuing your romantic interests and creative endeavors.

17 Wednesday

With the Moon moving into Leo, you may feel a heightened sense of self-expression and a desire to be seen and appreciated. Leo's influence brings a touch of dramatic flair to your emotions, and you might seek attention and recognition during this lunar transition. However, with Mercury opposing Saturn, you may encounter some communication challenges or feelings of mental restriction. This aspect can lead to self-doubt and a tendency to be overly critical.

18 Thursday

As Mercury moves into Libra, you may find yourself seeking more harmony and balance in your communication style. This astrological shift enhances your ability to see different perspectives and promotes fairness in your interactions. However, with Mercury opposed to Neptune, you may experience some challenges in thinking and decision-making. This aspect can create confusion, making it essential to be cautious about misunderstandings.

19 Friday

With Mercury forming trines to Uranus and Pluto, you may experience rising mental acuity and transformative insights. This astrological alignment stimulates your intellect and encourages you to think outside the box, embracing innovative ideas and alternative perspectives. Your communication skills are enhanced, and you may find it easier to express yourself with depth and clarity. It is an excellent time for problem-solving and research, as a thirst for knowledge fuels curiosity.

20 Saturday

When Venus forms a square aspect to Uranus, you may experience a period of unexpected disruptions and shifts in your relationships and emotions. This astrological influence can bring sudden changes in your love life, leading to feelings of restlessness and a desire for freedom and independence. While the Venus-Uranus square can ignite excitement and passion, it can also create tension and unpredictability in your interactions.

21 Sunday

As the Sun opposes Saturn, you may feel a sense of tension and limitations. This astrological aspect can bring obstacles that test your commitment to your goals. Being patient and disciplined during this period is essential, as overcoming setbacks and achieving your desired outcomes may require extra effort. Simultaneously, with the New Moon and the Moon's ingress into Libra, you have an opportunity for fresh beginnings and a focus on relationships and harmony.

22 Monday

As the Sun enters Libra, you are encouraged to seek fairness and cooperation in your relationships and endeavors. Libra's influence fosters a desire for peace and diplomacy, making it an excellent time to resolve conflicts and find a middle ground. Embrace the transformative energy of Mars in Scorpio, the equilibrium of the September Equinox, and the harmonious spirit of the Sun in Libra to cultivate self-discovery, growth, and balanced connections with those around you.

23 Tuesday

When the Sun opposes Neptune, you may experience heightened sensitivity and a blurred sense of reality. This astrological aspect can bring a sense of confusion and uncertainty, making it challenging to see things clearly and make sound judgments. You might be more susceptible to illusions or delusions, so be cautious of deceptive influences. You may also encounter challenges asserting yourself and understanding your true identity during this time.

24 Wednesday

With the Sun forming trines to Uranus and Pluto, you may experience a powerful transformative energy and innovation surge. This astrological alignment enhances your ability to embrace change and embrace your authentic self. Your confidence and sense of purpose heighten, making it an excellent time to take risks and pursue your goals fearlessly. As the Moon moves into Scorpio, your emotions become more intense and introspective.

25 Thursday

The news is imminent that provides a new option. It sees you approaching life with a boost in your step. It brings the motivation to develop your talents and grow your dreams. You embark on a chapter that is in alignment with your vision. Focusing on the essential steps needed to advance your abilities brings the start of something big. It helps you flex your wings and expand your horizons into new areas of interest.

26 Friday

Moon ingress Sagittarius's astrological influence encourages you to embrace a more adventurous and open-minded approach to life. You might strongly desire exploration and learning, seeking new experiences and opportunities to expand your horizons. The Sagittarius Moon fosters a spirit of freedom and independence, making it a favorable time to break from routine and engage in activities stimulating your mind and spirit.

27 Saturday

Serendipity graces your social life with uplifting news, creating a fortunate trend that opens doors to new people and social possibilities. The cosmic energies bring balance and harmony to your social interactions, fostering positive growth in your relationships. Embrace the lively exchanges and opportunities to mingle that accompany this news, emphasizing the improvement of your connections and cultivating a more vibrant and fulfilling social circle.

28 Sunday

Encouraging news breathes new life into your daily habits, offering a fortunate break to instigate positive changes in your lifestyle and overall well-being. This trend introduces balance and harmony into your daily activities, leading to noticeable improvements in your health and routines. Embrace the positive aspects as you navigate lively exchanges and opportunities to explore new wellness practices, cultivating a healthier and more harmonious lifestyle.

OCTOBER

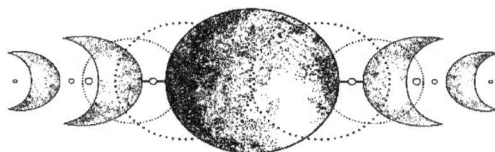

MOON MAGIC

Sun	Mon	Tue	Wed	Thu	Fri	Sat
			1	2	3	4
5	6	7	8	9	10	11
12	13	14	15	16	17	18
19	20	21	22	23	24	25
26	27	28	29	30	31	

NEW MOON

HUNTERS MOON

29 Monday

Moon ingress Capricorn astrological influence encourages you to approach your feelings in a more disciplined way. You might set ambitious goals and work diligently towards them. The Capricorn Moon's energy can require structure and order, prompting you to prioritize your responsibilities and long-term plans. Embrace this transit's practical and goal-oriented energy to make significant progress in your endeavors and lay the foundation for a stable and fulfilling future.

30 Tuesday

When discovering a treasure trove of opportunities, you hit a home run and head for a winning streak. You receive news that brings a boost into your world. It has a powerful effect as it provides a new landscape of options. It draws a happy shift forward that releases areas that have caused blocks and a lack of progress. Refining and streamlining your situation amplifies potential and enables you to turn and head toward growth.

1 Wednesday

As the Moon moves into Aquarius, you may experience a heightened sense of individuality and a desire to connect with others more intellectually. This astrological influence encourages you to embrace your unique perspectives and engage in conversations that expand your mind. However, with Mercury forming a square aspect to Jupiter, there's a potential for information overload and a tendency to exaggerate or overlook important details.

2 Thursday

A lucky twist amplifies your social life, creating a fortunate trend that opens doors to new people and social possibilities. The cosmic energies bring balance and harmony to your social interactions, fostering positive growth in your relationships. Embrace the lively exchanges and opportunities to mingle that accompany this news, emphasizing the improvement of your connections and cultivating a more vibrant and fulfilling social circle.

3 Friday

In the visionary eleventh house, your Libra Sun aligns with a desire for social harmony and collective goals. Your diplomatic and friendly nature makes you a natural connector within your social circles, fostering relationships based on shared values and mutual respect. You may find joy in group activities and collaborative projects that aim to create a more balanced and just society. Be mindful of the tendency to avoid confrontation at the expense of your convictions.

4 Saturday

Moon ingress Pisces astrological influence encourages you to connect with your inner world and the subtle energies around you. Pisces' energy fosters a sense of compassion and creativity, making it an ideal time for artistic expression and connecting with your emotions on a deeper level. During this lunar transit, you might find yourself drawn to reflective activities such as meditation, journaling, or simply daydreaming and reflecting.

5 Sunday

Joyful revelations unfold in your home and family life, ushering in a fortunate trend that opens doors to enhancements and growth. The cosmic energies introduce balance and harmony into your domestic sphere, emphasizing positive aspects that contribute to the overall well-being of your home life. Anticipate heartening news on the grapevine, providing room to strengthen familial bonds and create a more harmonious and joyful living environment.

6 Monday

As the Moon moves into Aries, you might experience a surge of energy and assertiveness. This astrological influence encourages you to take the initiative and enthusiastically pursue your goals. Aries' energy fosters a bold and courageous approach to your emotions, making it a time when you're more inclined to express yourself directly. Simultaneously, with Mercury entering Scorpio, your thinking becomes more profound and focused.

7 Tuesday

While the Full Moon illuminates your emotions, the Mercury-Pluto square might challenge your perception and push you to question your beliefs. Embrace the Full Moon's energy to release what no longer serves you while navigating the Mercury-Pluto square with mindfulness and a commitment to honest and respectful communication, allowing for transformation and growth in both your emotional and mental realms.

8 Wednesday

Venus sextile Jupiter is an excellent time for socializing and leisurely activities that bring joy and laughter. The Taurus Moon's energy enhances your sense of security, and Venus' alignment with Jupiter magnifies your feeling of love and abundance. Embrace this cosmic synergy to foster an understanding of contentment and make the most of this period of harmony and enjoyment in your connections and surroundings.

9 Thursday

Cosmic sparks inspire a surge of innovative creativity, unveiling a fortunate trend that broadens your artistic horizons. This positive news introduces balance and harmony into your creative pursuits, propelling growth and recognition for your unique talents. Immerse yourself in the momentum of lively exchanges and opportunities to collaborate with fellow creatives, creating an atmosphere of inspiration and nurturing the evolution of your creative expression.

10 Friday

As the Moon enters Gemini, you may notice a shift towards curiosity and mental engagement. This astrological influence encourages you to seek new information, engage in conversations, and explore various interests. Gemini's energy fosters versatility and adaptability, making it an ideal time to connect with others and share your thoughts and ideas. Your mind becomes more agile, and you might find yourself drawn to learning and exchanging knowledge.

11 Saturday

Venus opposed Saturn's astrological aspect, which can bring feelings of restriction and limitations in matters of love and connection. It's essential to be aware of any insecurities or fears that might arise and approach relationships with patience and a willingness to work through difficulties. This opposition encourages you to confront any barriers to intimacy or commitment, whether internal or external. This aspect also lets you reevaluate your values and priorities, fostering growth.

12 Sunday

Moon ingress Cancer. During this lunar transit, you might feel a more substantial need to protect and support those you care about. Embrace the Cancer Moon's energy to embrace your vulnerability and create a haven for yourself and those around you. This lunar aspect is an opportunity to delve into your emotions, find healing, and strengthen your connections by understanding the emotional bonds that tie us together.

13 Monday

Venus ingress Libra, you may notice a shift towards an emphasis on harmony. You might find yourself drawn to beauty and aesthetics, with an appreciation for art and culture. This transit can also enhance your social grace and charm, making it easier to build rapport with others. Embrace the Venus in Libra energy to cultivate meaningful relationships, foster a sense of unity, and create an atmosphere of peace and cooperation in both your personal and social spheres.

14 Tuesday

As Venus opposes Neptune, you may encounter a period of romantic idealism and potential for confusion in matters of the heart. This astrological aspect can bring a sense of longing and a tendency to see relationships through rose-colored glasses. However, with Pluto turning direct, transformative energy invites you to face truths. As the Moon moves into Leo, your emotions become more expressive and vibrant, encouraging you to seek creative outlets and bask in the spotlight.

15 Wednesday

A serendipitous windfall unfolds, impacting your daily work dynamics and offering an unexpected opportunity for positive change in your professional life. This trend opens doors to fresh strategies and possibilities, injecting a newfound sense of balance and harmony into your work environment. Embrace the positive aspects, signaling noticeable growth and advancement in your career. It ushers in lively exchanges and opportunities to collaborate with colleagues.

16 Thursday

As the Moon moves into Virgo, you may notice a shift towards practicality and attention to detail. This astrological influence encourages you to focus on organization and efficiency in your daily tasks and routines. Virgo's energy fosters a desire for cleanliness and order, making it an excellent time to tidy up your surroundings and take care of practical matters. During this lunar transit, you might find satisfaction in tackling projects that require precision and diligence.

17 Friday

Sun square Jupiter's astrological influence can bring a sense of expansion and a desire to take on new challenges. However, it's essential to be cautious of overconfidence or unrealistic expectations. This aspect can lead to a tendency to take on too much or to overlook details in your eagerness to pursue your goals. While the Sun-Jupiter square can boost your self-assurance and drive, it's essential to channel this energy wisely and avoid overextending yourself.

18 Saturday

Positive developments unfold in your home and family life, bringing a fortunate trend that opens doors to enhancements and growth. The cosmic energies introduce balance and harmony into your domestic sphere, emphasizing positive aspects that contribute to the overall well-being of your home life. Expect heartening news on the grapevine, providing room to strengthen familial bonds and create a more harmonious and joyful living environment.

19 Sunday

With the Moon moving into Libra, you may experience a shift towards a greater focus on harmony and relationships. This astrological transition encourages you to seek balance and fairness in your interactions with others. Libra's energy fosters a desire for companionship and a willingness to compromise to create harmonious connections. You might seek aesthetics, art, and activities that bring joy and pleasure during this lunar transit.

20 Monday

Mercury conjunct Mars astrological alignment intensifies your communication style, making your thoughts and ideas more direct and persuasive. Your mind becomes sharper and more focused, allowing you to tackle tasks with confidence and clarity. However, be mindful of the potential for impulsive speech or rushed decisions. The Mercury-Mars conjunction can foster a dynamic approach to problem-solving, making it excellent for initiating projects.

21 Tuesday

New Moon. Moon ingress Scorpio. During a New Moon, you may feel a sense of fresh beginnings and the opportunity to set new intentions. This astrological phase represents a clean slate and a chance to plant seeds for future growth. As the Moon moves into Scorpio, your emotions may become more intense and introspective. Scorpio's energy encourages you to delve deep within yourself, allowing you to explore your inner motivations and desires.

22 Wednesday

Neptune ingress Pisces astrological shift encourages you to foster empathy and compassion, urging you to tap into the universal energies that connect us all. During this transit, you might find yourself drawn to artistic pursuits, meditation, and activities that allow you to escape the boundaries of the everyday world. Embrace the Neptune-Pisces connection to dive into the depths of your inner world and let your intuition guide a journey of self-discovery and spiritual growth.

23 Thursday

As the Sun moves into Scorpio, you may notice a shift towards more intense and transformative energy. This astrological transition encourages you to delve deeper into your emotions and embrace a sense of empowerment. Scorpio's energy fosters a desire for authenticity and a willingness to confront hidden truths. It is a favorable time to explore your innermost desires and face any aspects of yourself that may need healing and renewal.

24 Friday

With the Moon moving into Sagittarius, you may experience adventurous curiosity and a desire for exploration. This astrological shift encourages new experiences and expands your horizons. However, the Sun's square to Pluto can bring intensity and potential power struggles. It's essential to navigate this aspect with mindfulness and avoid overcontrolling. On a brighter note, Mercury's trine to Jupiter enhances your communication skills and intellectual prowess.

25 Saturday

When Mercury forms a trine with Saturn, you may experience a period of enhanced mental clarity and disciplined thinking. This astrological alignment empowers you to focus on practical matters and approach your tasks precisely. Your communication becomes more structured and organized, making it an ideal time for planning, studying, and engaging in tasks requiring attention to detail. It's an excellent time for complex tasks as your concentration heightens.

26 Sunday

As the Moon moves into Capricorn, you may notice a shift towards a more disciplined and goal-oriented emotional state. This astrological influence encourages you to approach your feelings with responsibility and determination. Capricorn's energy fosters a desire for practicality and achievement, making it an excellent time to focus on tasks that require focus and commitment. During this lunar transit, you might crave activities contributing to long-term objectives.

27 Monday

Brace yourself for a paradigm shift in your professional landscape as unfolding revelations bring unforeseen prospects and constructive shifts to your daily work regimen. This emerging trend unfurls opportunities for novel strategies, infusing newfound equilibrium and harmony into your workspace. Engage in spirited exchanges and cooperative ventures with colleagues, injecting dynamism into your workplace and fostering an energetic and flourishing ambiance.

28 Tuesday

When Mars forms a trine aspect to Jupiter, you may experience a period of heightened enthusiasm and an expansive drive to take action. This astrological alignment amplifies your confidence and energy levels, encouraging you to pursue your goals with vigor. Your assertiveness aligns with a sense of optimism and belief in your abilities. This trine inspires you to tackle challenges with a positive attitude and a willingness to take calculated risks.

29 Wednesday

As the Moon moves into Aquarius, you may notice a more independent and forward-thinking outlook. This astrological transition encourages you to embrace your uniqueness and connect with like-minded individuals who share your innovative ideas. With Mercury forming a trine to Neptune, your thoughts and communication may take on a dreamy and imaginative quality. This aspect fosters creativity and intuitive insights, making it a favorable time for artistic pursuits.

30 Thursday

Mercury sextile Pluto. This sextile encourages you to engage in meaningful discussions and seek information that can lead to personal growth and understanding. You might find yourself drawn to research and investigation, allowing you to uncover layers of complexity that were previously unseen. Embrace the Mercury-Pluto sextile's energy to foster intellectual growth and connect with others on a deeper level.

NOVEMBER

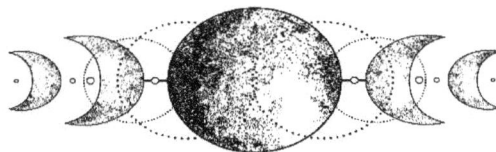

MOON MAGIC

Sun	Mon	Tue	Wed	Thu	Fri	Sat
						1
2	3	4	5	6	7	8
9	10	11	12	13	14	15
16	17	18	19	20	21	22
23	24	25	26	27	28	29
30						

New Moon

BEAVER MOON

31 Friday

As the Moon moves into Pisces, you may notice heightened emotional sensitivity and a greater connection to your intuitive side. This astrological transition encourages you to embrace your imagination and explore your feelings. Pisces' energy fosters a sense of empathy and compassion, urging you to connect with others on a more soulful and understanding level. During this lunar transit, you might explore artistic or creative activities that allow you to express emotions.

1 Saturday

With the Sun illuminating your twelfth house, your Scorpio energy takes on a more mysterious and reflective quality. Your probing nature is turned inward, leading to a deep exploration of your subconscious and spiritual realms. You may find solace in practices such as meditation or psychology, allowing you to navigate the hidden aspects of your psyche. Be mindful of the potential for emotional intensity, and seek healthy outlets for self-discovery and healing.

2 Sunday

With the Moon moving into Aries, you may experience a surge of energy and a desire for action. This astrological transition encourages you to embrace a more assertive approach. Aries' energy fosters a sense of independence and a willingness to tackle challenges head-on. However, with Venus squaring Jupiter, there's a potential for overindulgence and impractical optimism in matters of the heart. This aspect can bring forth a tendency to overextend or overlook potential pitfalls.

3 Monday

Unexpectedly good news brings a fortunate twist to your daily work dynamics, offering a golden opportunity for positive change. This trend unlocks new strategies and possibilities, infusing balance and harmony into your work environment. Embrace the positive aspects that promise noticeable growth and advancement in your career. The news also ushers in opportunities to collaborate with colleagues, creating a vibrant and flourishing workplace.

4 Tuesday

With Mars forming a trine to Neptune, you may experience a period of heightened creativity and a harmonious blend of action and intuition. This astrological alignment empowers you to pursue your goals with inspired imagination. As Mars moves into Sagittarius, your actions become more driven by a desire for exploration and adventure. Simultaneously, the Moon's ingress into Taurus focuses on stability and sensory pleasures.

5 Wednesday

During a Full Moon, you may experience a heightened sense of culmination and realization. This astrological phase encourages you to assess your progress and achievements. It's a time of heightened emotions and increased awareness as the illumination of the Full Moon reveals your life's successes and challenges. This phase invites you to reflect on your intentions during the previous New Moon and make any necessary adjustments.

6 Thursday

Mars sextile Pluto astrological alignment empowers you to tap into your inner strength and make focused strides towards your goals. As the Moon moves into Gemini, your emotions become more curious and adaptable, fostering a desire for intellectual stimulation and diverse experiences. Simultaneously, as Venus enters Scorpio, your relationships and romantic desires may become more intense and passionate.

7 Friday

Serendipity graces your social life with uplifting news, creating a fortunate trend that opens doors to new people and social possibilities. The cosmic energies bring balance and harmony to your social interactions, fostering positive growth in your relationships. Embrace the lively exchanges and opportunities to mingle that accompany this news, emphasizing the improvement of your connections and cultivating a more vibrant and fulfilling social circle.

8 Saturday

With the Moon moving into Cancer, your emotions become more nurturing and sensitive, urging you to seek comfort and connection. Embrace the Uranus-Taurus energy to explore uncharted territories while using the Venus-Pluto square as an opportunity to confront any unhealthy patterns. The Moon's transit in Cancer encourages you to find solace in emotional bonds, providing support and understanding as you navigate this period of shifts and emotional depth.

9 Sunday

When Mercury turns retrograde, you may experience a period of introspection and review in communication and decision-making. This astrological phenomenon can bring forth a need to reevaluate your plans, revisit past conversations, and pay attention to overlooked details. Miscommunications and misunderstandings might be more common during this time, urging you to practice patience and clear communication.

10 Monday

Moon ingress Leo. During this lunar transit, you might find yourself drawn to activities that allow you to showcase your talents and receive positive attention. It is a favorable time to engage in social interactions, express yourself authentically, and enjoy moments of playful self-expression. Embrace the Leo Moon's energy to celebrate your uniqueness, share your passions with others, and find joy in connecting with increased confidence and vibrant emotional energy.

11 Tuesday

As Jupiter turns retrograde, you may experience a period of internal reflection and reassessment of your growth and expansion. This astrological shift encourages you to look within and review your beliefs, goals, and long-term plans. While Jupiter's retrograde motion can sometimes bring a temporary slowdown in external progress, it also offers an opportunity to gain deeper insights into your aspirations. It's a time to examine whether your path aligns with your values.

12 Wednesday

Mercury conjunct Mars astrological alignment empowers you with assertive and direct communication skills. Your thoughts become quick and decisive, encouraging you to take initiative and express yourself clearly. As the Moon moves into Virgo, your emotions may focus more on details and practical matters. This combination of energies invites you to engage in productive conversations and tackle tasks that require attention to precision.

13 Thursday

Advancing your abilities into new areas enables you to achieve valuable results. Your efforts give you a remarkable degree of advancement that has you thinking about the possibilities in a new light. It brings new pathways and options to light. Taking on more responsibilities and challenges puts you in good stead to refine and level up your skills. Your expertise is valued and brings a pleasing result for your working life.

14 Friday

Improvements flow into your life that connect you with others who support your growth. It sparks a time of sharing thoughts and ideas as you connect with friends. The scene is social, discussions are animated, and the pace is lively. Exciting opportunities to mingle with companions are ready to roll into your life. It touches you down on a prosperous journey by catching up with kindred spirits. You make progress on all levels, personal and professional.

15 Saturday

Moon ingress Libra. Libra's energy fosters a desire for companionship and a willingness to find common ground. During this lunar transition, you might find yourself drawn to social activities and engaging in conversations that create understanding and unity. Your appreciation for beauty and aesthetics may also heighten, inspiring you to enjoy your surroundings and engage in creative pursuits.

16 Sunday

Upbeat news disrupts your daily habits positively, offering a fortunate break to instigate changes in your lifestyle and overall well-being. This trend introduces balance and harmony into your daily activities, leading to noticeable improvements in your health and routines. Embrace the positive aspects as you navigate lively exchanges and opportunities to explore new wellness practices, promoting a healthier and more harmonious lifestyle.

17 Monday

With the Sun forming trines to Jupiter and Saturn, you may experience balanced and constructive energy. This astrological alignment empowers you with a harmonious blend of expansion and discipline. Your confidence and optimism align well with your ability to make practical and strategic decisions. As Mercury sextiles Pluto, your communication gains depth and insight, allowing you to engage in meaningful conversations that lead to transformative outcomes.

18 Tuesday

Celestial inspirations infuse your creative endeavors with innovative energy, unveiling a fortunate trend that expands your artistic horizons. This positive news draws balance and harmony into your creative pursuits, propelling growth and recognition for your unique talents. Anticipate lively exchanges and opportunities to collaborate with fellow creatives, creating an atmosphere of inspiration and fostering the evolution of your creative expression.

19 Wednesday

As Mercury moves into Scorpio, your thoughts and communication may take on a more profound tone. This astrological transition encourages you to delve into deeper layers of your mind and explore complex subjects. However, with Mercury opposed to Uranus, there's potential for sudden shifts in your thinking and unexpected disruptions in your communication. This aspect can bring innovative ideas and challenges in coherently conveying your thoughts.

20 Thursday

During a New Moon, you may experience a sense of fresh beginnings and opportunities. This astrological phase marks a time to set intentions and initiate new projects. With the Sun conjunct Mercury, your thoughts and communication align closely with your personal goals. As Mercury moves into Sagittarius, your thinking becomes expansive and open to exploration. The Uranus sextile Neptune aspect adds innovative creativity and spiritual insight to your endeavors.

21 Friday

As the Sun opposes Uranus, you may encounter unexpected changes and disruptions. This astrological aspect can bring about a sense of restlessness and a desire for freedom from limitations. Embrace this time as an opportunity to break free from routines that no longer serve you and to embrace a more authentic expression of yourself. On the other hand, the Sun's trine to Neptune adds a touch of dreamy and intuitive energy to your experiences.

22 Saturday

Embrace the Sagittarius Sun's energy to embrace new experiences and the spirit of exploration. Use the Mercury-Saturn trine to communicate effectively and make well-considered decisions. Let the Capricorn Moon's influence inspire you to tackle tasks with determination, allow the Mercury-Jupiter trine to fuel your intellectual pursuits, and encourage you to think big as you navigate this dynamic and productive period.

23 Sunday

With the Sun forming a sextile to Pluto, you may experience a period of increased personal empowerment and transformative potential. This astrological alignment empowers you with determination and the ability to delve deep into matters that require your attention. This aspect encourages you to embrace change and tap into your inner strength, fostering a sense of renewal and personal growth. This cosmic synergy harnesses your inner power for self-discovery and transformation.

24 Monday

You nurture an area that inspires growth. A wave of information arrives that takes you towards change. You may decide to switch lanes and grow your talents and abilities. Putting the shine on your skills lets you merge with opportunity. Game-changing information sweeps you towards a dynamic chapter of growing a worthwhile area. It enables you to craft a beautiful journey that resonates with abundance.

25 Tuesday

With Mercury forming a conjunction with Venus, you may experience a period of enhanced communication and social harmony. This astrological alignment empowers you with a charming and diplomatic approach to interactions. Your thoughts and conversations infuse with elegance and grace. As the Moon moves into Aquarius, your emotions may become more attuned to a sense of independence and open-mindedness.

26 Wednesday

Venus trines Jupiter. Venus trine Saturn. This combination suggests that you may enjoy meaningful and lasting connections and build trust and commitment. Embrace these Venus trines' energy to enhance your relationships and creative endeavors. Allow the blend of enthusiasm and stability to guide you towards a balanced approach to matters of the heart, fostering a sense of growth and enduring connection in your sphere.

27 Thursday

On Thanksgiving, as the Moon moves into Pisces, you may find an atmosphere of heightened emotional connection. This astrological transition encourages you to embrace the spirit of gratitude and empathy for the people around you and the blessings in your life. Pisces' energy fosters a sense of sensitivity and a desire to create an atmosphere of warmth and understanding. It's a time to appreciate the company of loved ones and reflect on the holiday's significance.

28 Friday

Saturn's direct astrological event marks a time when the energy of Saturn, which represents structure and discipline, begins to move more steadily in its natural forward direction. It's a favorable period for making concrete plans and taking practical steps to achieve your ambitions. Saturn's direct motion can bring a sense of accountability and focus to your endeavors, allowing you to address any lingering issues or obstacles with determination.

29 Saturday

Mercury's direct astrological event marks the end of a period where communication, travel, and decision-making may have felt more tangled or delayed. As Mercury moves forward, it's an excellent time to implement the insights and revisions you've made during its retrograde phase. You'll likely find that information flows more smoothly, making it easier to express yourself and make informed choices.

30 Sunday

Moon ingress Aries astrological shift encourages you to embrace independence and enthusiastically pursue your desires. However, with Venus opposed to Uranus, there's potential for disruptions or unexpected changes in matters of the heart and personal values. The Venus trine Neptune aspect adds a touch of romance and creativity to your relationships, balancing the unpredictability of the opposition.

December

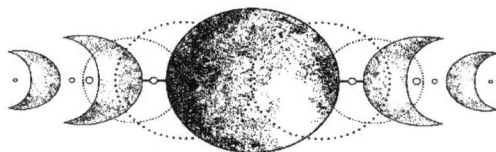

MOON MAGIC

Sun	Mon	Tue	Wed	Thu	Fri	Sat
	1	2	3	4	5	6
7	8	9	10	11	12	13
14	15	16	17	18	19	20
21	22	23	24	25	26	27
28	29	30	31			

NEW MOON

_____

_____

_____

_____

_____

_____

_____

_____

_____

_____

_____

_____

_____

_____

_____

_____

_____

_____

_____

_____

_____

COLD MOON

1 Monday

Exciting news brings about promising changes in your daily work routine, offering a fortunate break to initiate positive shifts in your professional life. This trend opens doors to new strategies and possibilities, injecting a sense of balance into your work environment. Embrace the positive aspects that signal noticeable advancement in your career. The news also brings lively exchanges and opportunities to collaborate with colleagues, fostering a thriving workplace.

2 Tuesday

Embrace the Taurus Moon's energy to indulge in self-care and appreciate the beauty around you while allowing the Venus-Pluto sextile to inspire you to nurture your relationships with a sense of depth and authenticity. This combination invites you to create a harmonious and fulfilling atmosphere that resonates with comfort and emotional intensity as you navigate this period of sensual and transformative energies.

3 Wednesday

Uplifting news initiates a fortunate shift in your daily work routine, offering a lucky break to create positive changes in your professional life. This trend opens doors to new approaches and possibilities, introducing a sense of balance and harmony to your work environment. Embrace the positive aspects that promise noticeable growth and advancement in your career—lively exchanges and opportunities to collaborate with colleagues, contributing to a thriving workplace.

4 Thursday

With the Moon moving into Gemini and a Full Moon on the horizon, you may find emotions and thoughts are heightened in awareness and clarity. This astrological phase marks a culmination, where the intentions during the previous New Moon come to fruition. The energy of Gemini encourages curiosity and a desire to engage in meaningful conversations and exchanges of information. This Full Moon is an opportune time to reflect on your progress and achievements.

5 Friday

Things are on the move for your social life. Changes ahead open a new life cycle. Sharing with kindred spirits becomes part of your routine as a more extensive phase of progress opens life up. It puts you in contact with others who bring a valuable sense of support and connection into your world. It rules a time of increasing expansion and harmony. It creates foundations that offer room to grow your circle of friends.

6 Saturday

With the Moon moving into Cancer, this astrological transition encourages you to seek comfort in familiar surroundings and connect with your feelings on a deeper level. Cancer's energy fosters a strong desire for emotional security and a tendency to be more attuned to the needs of yourself and those close to you. Additionally, Mercury's formation of a trine with Neptune makes your communication and thoughts more intuitive and imaginative.

7 Sunday

Celestial inspirations fuel creative momentum, unveiling a fortunate trend that broadens your artistic horizons. This positive news introduces balance and harmony into your creative pursuits, propelling growth and recognition for your unique talents. You can look forward to lively exchanges and opportunities to collaborate with fellow creatives, creating an atmosphere of inspiration and nurturing the evolution of your creative expression.

8 Monday

Unexpected news brings a journey that offers a dynamic time field with possibilities. It opens the path to luck and optimism. It brings expansion that hits a high note for your social life as it enables you to make notable tracks on improving the foundations of your life. A big reveal is coming; expanding your life becomes a priority, connecting you with others with similar goals. Essential changes draw a time that offers happiness and abundance.

9 Tuesday

With Mars forming a square to Saturn, you might encounter frustration and obstacles in your endeavors. This astrological aspect can bring about a sense of restriction and delays in your actions and plans. Being patient and persistent during this time is essential, as the Mars-Saturn square tests your determination and resilience. Instead of rushing headlong into challenges, consider a more structured and thoughtful approach to overcoming them.

10 Wednesday

Moon ingress Virgo astrological transition encourages you to pay attention to the practical aspects of your life and attend to matters with precision and organization. Virgo's energy fosters a desire for efficiency and a keen eye for detail. Additionally, with Neptune turning direct, you may feel a subtle shift in your dreams, intuition, and spiritual pursuits. This cosmic event brings a sense of clarity to your inner world, allowing you to move forward with greater insight.

11 Thursday

With Mercury forming a trine to Neptune, you may experience a period of heightened intuition and imaginative thinking. This astrological alignment empowers you with a more profound connection to your inner world and a greater receptivity to the subtle aspects of life. Your communication and thoughts take on a compassionate and empathetic quality, making it an ideal time for creative endeavors and spiritual pursuits.

12 Friday

As the Moon gracefully moves into Libra, you may sense a desire for harmony and balance. This astrological transition encourages you to seek fairness and equilibrium in your interactions and surroundings. Libra's energy fosters a deep appreciation for aesthetics and diplomacy, making it a favorable time to engage in activities that promote peace and beauty. Your social side may emerge, drawing you toward pleasant conversations and cooperative endeavors.

13 Saturday

Mercury sextile Pluto. You may find that your capacity for strategic thinking and problem-solving is heightened during this time. Use the Mercury-Pluto sextile to engage in conversations that have a transformative impact and dive into study or research areas that captivate your curiosity. Allow this cosmic synergy to guide you in expressing your thoughts and ideas with depth and precision as you navigate this mental empowerment and discovery period.

14 Sunday

With Mars forming a square to Neptune, you might experience uncertainty in your actions and desires. This astrological aspect can bring a foggy quality to your motivations, making it challenging to define your goals or assert yourself confidently. It's as if the energy of Mars, associated with assertiveness and determination, is tangled up in Neptune's dreamy and elusive realm. During this period, you may find it beneficial to take a step back and reassess your plans.

15 Monday

As the Moon moves into Scorpio and Mars enters Capricorn, you might feel your drive and ambition boost. This astrological transition can bring about a sense of determination and resilience in your actions. Scorpio's energy encourages you to delve into your innermost feelings and desires, making it a suitable time for introspection and transformation. With Mars in Capricorn, you'll likely find your motivation and goals more structured and goal-oriented.

16 Tuesday

An exciting journey ahead fills in the blanks. It starts a new trend in your life that migrates away from difficulties as you embark on making the most of an influx of options that grow your abilities. It puts you on a course to advance your talents and deepen your knowledge. Working with your skills builds stable foundations that offer success and prosperity. It helps you unlock a brighter path that ushers in rising possibilities for your career.

17 Wednesday

With the Sun forming a square to Saturn, you might encounter challenges and limitations in your pursuits. This astrological aspect can bring a sense of restriction and the need to confront responsibilities or obstacles that stand in your way. It's as if you're facing a test of your patience and determination. However, as the Moon moves into Sagittarius, there's a shift in the emotional atmosphere, encouraging you to seek adventure and a broader perspective.

18 Thursday

Experience a serendipitous twist deepening your social life, creating a fortunate trend that opens doors to new people and social possibilities. The cosmic energies bring balance and harmony to your social interactions, fostering positive growth in your relationships. Embrace the lively exchanges and opportunities to mingle that accompany this news, emphasizing the improvement of your connections and cultivating a more vibrant and fulfilling social circle.

19 Friday

Upbeat news disrupts your daily habits in a positive light, presenting a fortunate break to instigate changes in your lifestyle and overall well-being. This trend introduces balance and harmony into your daily activities, leading to noticeable improvements in your health and routines. Embrace the positive aspects as you navigate lively exchanges and opportunities to explore new wellness practices, fostering a healthier and more harmonious lifestyle.

20 Saturday

The Black Moon entering Sagittarius adds a layer of introspection and a quest for knowledge and understanding. Embrace this cosmic alignment as an opportunity to set personal and spiritual growth intentions while using the Capricorn Moon's energy to ground your efforts in practicality and determination. Allow the influence of the Black Moon in Sagittarius to inspire a sense of adventure and a quest for wisdom as you navigate this period of new beginnings and self-discovery.

21 Sunday

As the Sun forms a square to Neptune, you might find confusion or uncertainty clouding your vision. This astrological aspect can bring moments of doubt or illusion, making it essential to be cautious with decision-making and clarity of intent. Simultaneously, with Venus squaring Saturn, you could encounter challenges in the heart or finances. It's a time when commitments and responsibilities may weigh heavily on your relationships and wallet.

22 Monday

As the Moon moves into Aquarius, you may sense a shift towards a more open-minded and socially conscious state of mind. This astrological transition encourages you to embrace individuality and express your unique perspective. Aquarius' energy fosters a desire for innovation and a strong sense of community. You might find yourself drawn to unconventional ideas and approaches and feel more inclined to connect with like-minded individuals who share your vision.

23 Tuesday

New options arrive, which bring a lift to your social life. A pathway ahead develops your life's journey, and you can trust your instincts to guide you correctly. Lighter energy helps you build stable foundations that secure a pleasing result. It ushers in a time for networking and mingling with friends. You land in a supportive environment that links with heightened social engagement. Magic courses through your life, bringing a theme of improving your circumstances.

24 Wednesday

With Venus forming a square to Neptune, you may encounter a period of emotional complexity and potential illusions in matters of the heart. This astrological aspect can bring about confusion and a tendency to see things through rose-colored glasses. However, as Venus transitions into Capricorn, you'll find a growing emphasis on practicality and responsibility in your romantic and financial endeavors.

25 Thursday

As the Moon gracefully enters Pisces on Christmas Day, you might experience a heightened sense of compassion, imagination, and emotional connection. This astrological shift encourages you to embrace the season's spirit, focusing on the warmth of love and the joy of giving. Pisces' energy fosters a deep emotional sensitivity and a desire to connect with the intangible, creating a dreamy and spiritual atmosphere.

26 Friday

Serendipity graces your social life with uplifting news, creating a fortunate trend that opens doors to new people and social possibilities. The cosmic energies bring balance and harmony to your social interactions, fostering positive growth in your relationships. Embrace the lively exchanges and opportunities to mingle that accompany this news, emphasizing the improvement of your connections and cultivating a more vibrant and fulfilling social circle.

27 Saturday

Moon ingress Aries astrological shift encourages you to take initiative and pursue your desires with enthusiasm and courage. Aries' energy fosters a sense of independence and a willingness to blaze new trails. You may find yourself feeling more self-assured and ready to tackle challenges head-on. It's a favorable time to start new projects, assert your needs, and embrace a spirit of boldness. Use this cosmic influence to channel your inner drive and adopt a "can-do" attitude.

28 Sunday

Positive developments unfold in your home and family life, ushering in a fortunate trend that opens doors to enhancements and growth. The cosmic energies introduce balance and harmony into your domestic sphere, emphasizing positive aspects that contribute to the overall well-being of your home life. Anticipate heartening news on the grapevine, providing room to strengthen familial bonds and create a more harmonious and joyful living environment.

29 Monday

Moon ingress Taurus. During this time, you might find solace in the simple joys of good food, soothing music, or the beauty of nature. Use this cosmic influence to create a serene and nurturing environment for yourself and indulge in life's little luxuries. The Taurus Moon invites you to slow down, savor the moment, and appreciate the tangible aspects of your existence, allowing you to find emotional stability and contentment in the here and now.

30 Tuesday

When Mercury squares Saturn, you may face challenges related to communication and decision-making. Your thoughts and ideas might encounter obstacles or delays, making it harder to express yourself clearly or make quick judgments. It can feel as though your mental processes are under constant scrutiny, leading to self-doubt and caution in your verbal and written interactions. Work on honing communication skills and developing a structured approach.

31 Wednesday

As New Year's Eve unfolds and the Moon moves into the sign of Gemini, you may feel curious and social energy. Your emotions may become more adaptable and changeable, much like the quicksilver nature of Gemini. This transition can bring a desire for lighthearted conversations, mingling with various people, and exploring new ideas and experiences. You might feel drawn to engage in festive gatherings, enjoying the company of friends as you usher in the new year.

1 Thursday

On New Year's Day, Mercury's ingress into Capricorn combines with a challenging square aspect to Neptune, creating an intriguing blend of practicality and potential confusion in your thinking and communication. You may start the year with a more grounded and goal-oriented mindset, focusing on your ambitions and responsibilities. However, the square to Neptune can introduce some haziness or unrealistic thinking into your plans and conversations.

Astrology, Tarot & Horoscope Books.

Mystic Cat

Mystic Cat Tarot

In Relationship Reading

$15.00

Crossroads

$10.00

Next Relationship Reading

$15.00

Ohoroscope@Hotmail.com

www.ingramcontent.com/pod-product-compliance
Lightning Source LLC
Chambersburg PA
CBHW080530090426
42733CB00015B/2544